Houses for Aging Socially

Developing Third Place Ecologies

University of Arkansas Community Design Center

By 2030, 79 million Baby Boomers will have turned 65 at a rate of 10,000 per day. While more than 85 percent will age in place, a tsunami of challenges and opportunities will compel this cohort to embrace more cooperative structures of living, given their explosive increase in single-person households. Predicted shortages in social services and healthcare labor—some anticipating a nursing shortfall in the hundreds of thousands by 2030—will limit access to necessary long-term services and supports; this too will encourage greater interdependence. Lack of adequate financial preparation among Boomers compared to their predecessors will encourage new economies of sharing. Alarmingly, 55 percent of households in which the head is over 55 will have to rely almost entirely on Social Security income, a program itself under stress. Moreover, the nation's housing stock and neighborhoods are not equipped to serve the common mobility, access, and social needs of seniors. Many who now age in place, often experience greater social isolation and loss of purpose than residents of nursing homes. *Third Place Ecologies* proposes new types of housing fabrics that promote informal social and economic entrepreneurship in neighborhoods once resistant to such development. Design approaches consider ordinary components of the standard single-family house—porches, garages, lawns, courts, terraces, gardens/gardensheds, and garages/workshops—that may be recast in collective field conditions. What new place-making solutions can this vocabulary generate that allows seniors to thrive beyond a simple aging in place?

Content

Introduction: Housing as a Social Context for Aging 8
Stephen Luoni

A Gerontological Framework for New Senior Living Models 13
Alexis Denton

Shared Space and the Shared Economy 17
Thomas Fisher

Place in Aging: A Brief Note on Michael Haneke's *Amour* 21
Daniel Friedman

Rethinking Aging and Housing 28

Why Aging? Why so Disruptive? 36

City+Culture 44

Introducing Third Place Fabrics 48
    Hyper-porch 52
    Patio Mat 76
    Garage Gallery 100

Retrofitting Existing Fabric 130

End Notes and Image Credits 138

Studies show that people with strong social relationships increased their survival odds by 50 percent over a certain time period, equivalent to giving up smoking and nearly twice as beneficial as physical activity.

Freeman, South Dakota, 1880s

Introduction: Housing as a Social Context for Aging

Stephen Luoni

"A decent life for the old cannot, in most cases, be financed by individuals."
Susan Jacoby, *Never Say Die: The Myth and Marketing of the New Old Age*

Aging as a morphing social construction is prompting new thinking on current forms of housing. Since the rise of post-WWII prosperity, American culture uniquely projected new ideals of independence onto aging, celebrating detachment from work, family, and community. Leisure-based lifestyles associated with expanded lifespan—the "longevity dividend"—paralleled private sector development of pensions, retirement communities, and a professionalized senior caregiving industry. The latter relieved family members from having to exhaust their own savings and career opportunities to provide full-time care when the need arose among their elders. Notwithstanding this widespread mediatization of retirement, such lifestyle turns out to be true for less than ten percent of the senior population.

Updated constructions of aging, like the optimistic "successful aging" go beyond leisure to imagine freedom from infirmity and even the prospect of agelessness with the right lifestyle. At its minimum, successful aging highlights the role of personal reinvention, so prized by the Baby Boom generation in their navigation of adulthood. Meanwhile, the more fatalist "deficit model" forecasts widespread declines in access to health care and the few aging-supportive residential environments remaining—just as the 65-plus population doubles in number over the next generation. Public sector and institutional safety nets developed during previous generations have become overwhelmed by high costs and widening scales of need for services.

How, then, will retiring Boomers reshape the future of aging? Emerging grassroots initiatives on "aging in community" (as opposed to aging in place) are substituting local support systems for reliance on formal sector services. The latter's medical model employs costly management-centric solutions even when low impact social remedies would knowingly yield better outcomes. New approaches to aging in community—and other pressing social challenges for that matter—will involve smaller scales and deeper social relationships. Attention is turning to housing as a context for bundling community-based services into everyday living. Indeed, housing may be the singular most important platform for developing synergistic approaches to livability challenges that often worsen with aging—including poverty, declining health, and social isolation.

Reclaiming Informality in Living Environments

Most housing fails to serve the physical and social needs unique to aging. The dominant housing model—outside of America's urban centers—encodes homeowner autonomy through distance from neighbors and segregation from non-residential land uses. Suburban concepts of place favored automobile use over development of public transit and good town form, both structured around walkable access to essential services. Nearly sixty-two percent of America's housing stock is single-family detached housing created for the child-centered nuclear family. Yet, this household structure will constitute only 14 percent of all household formation over the next generation. Nevertheless, four generations of Americans were raised in auto-dominant settings, including seniors who now age in place, creating the fastest growing default residential environment—Naturally Occurring Retirement Communities, or NORCs.

Many who prize independence by aging in place (or grow stuck in place due to finances) eventually find their conventional single-family homes lack ready adaptability to their changing needs. The typical floor plan is often multi-level and inflexible, over-determined by small cellular spaces that are unaccommodating of wheelchair use and general ease in mobility. Outdoor landscapes, designed as buffers requiring constant upkeep fortress the home and inhibit social exchange among neighbors. The American home was driven by what architectural historian, Niklas Maak, calls a "pathology of privacy." Meanwhile, studies show that aging populations fear social isolation and loss of purpose more than death. Unwittingly, their homes become independence traps. Impediments to their well-being only to be exacerbated by subdivisions equally resistant to evolution with shifting needs. The longevity economy will likely disrupt such fixed notions of housing, fulfilling Maak's optimism that "the private and public are not basic anthropological constants either, but rather historically established concepts subject to social and technological change."

Perhaps the best advice for prosperous aging is to move to a city. Yet, despite urbanists' predictions for a post-recession boom in urban multi-family housing starts, Americans still favor (80 percent) single-family detached housing, though they wish for urban amenities presently absent. Nonetheless, single-family housing fabrics can be retooled as neighborhood support systems, especially with the emergence of informal peer-to-peer networks. Pop-up sharing economies aided by social media stimulate post-retirement work and neighborhood-based exchanges of goods and services related to transportation, home improvement, errand fulfillment, landscaping, and domestic assistance. Shared makerspaces and other co-working environments encourage start-up hobby or income-producing activities without significant capital costs. Through emergent co-housing initiatives and resident-centric organizations like the Village network, Boomers are structuring home-based care economies around the provision of mutual support for the most common non-medical impairments in walking, cooking, and toilet functioning—what gerontologists call ADLs (activities of daily living). Such informal arrangements breed resilience, a measure of the social capital necessary to thrive in the face of obstacles and disruptions wrought by longevity. Informality as an economic and social force historically conditioned neighborhood prosperity, and could again if we reimagined residential environments as contexts with deep social functioning beyond the fortressed household.

American neighborhoods once sponsored a diverse spectrum of adaptable housing products. Co-housing, pocket neighborhoods, and the spectrum of pre-1940s "missing middle housing"—bungalow courts, townhouses, patio homes, two-over-twos, maisonettes, multiplexes, garage apartments, etc.—evidenced a rich history of placemaking with moderate-to-low-density housing. Mostly abandoned by the formal banking sector—hence missing middle—these real estate products intermingled work, leisure, and residential uses through a complex ecology of public and private spaces. This particularly American form of neighborhood-making encouraged spontaneous economies, mythologizing successful garage start-ups that became corporate titans. Neighborhoods before

Euclidean zoning (single land use) generated surplus social and entrepreneurial capital, a complexity that has since been regulated out of existence. By the mid-20th century, diversity in household structures and neighborhoods had been replaced by homogeneity in subdivisions, the latter lacking the interconnectedness that underwrites vital social life.

Our study, however, does not attempt to reconstitute the traditional neighborhood, but instead stimulate new communal possibilities using current forms of housing. The study recasts the single-family home's private frontage as communal frameworks for hosting activities beyond the household. Rethinking the porch, garage, and lawn-cum-patio as shared frameworks challenges the social and economic entropy in subdivision development, the site of most NORCs. Immediate and novel communal forms—"third places"—can be derived from expanding the latent potential in the porch, garage, or patio. What is a third place?

Rooms that Grow a City

Coined by urban sociologist, Ray Oldenburg, the third place is neither home nor work, but rather the liminal space in cities—clubs, cafes, taverns, barber shops, and parks—where civil exchanges, particularly artful conversation, are continually enacted. Applying notions of liminality (in-betweenness) to housing, imagine the impact of a porch, ordinarily a room, rescaled to an entire block. Recalling Archigram's plug-in city, various housing types would plug into the porch armature, allowing residents to socialize in what becomes a shared clubhouse. This successional version of the porch sponsors a multi-layered system of screened rooms, patios, and open decks where residents can enjoy greater community and privacy simultaneously.

Likewise, consider the garage a neighborhood makerspace or salon, like Latin American immigrants who convert garages to public markets and neighborhood drink stations. Perhaps garages should be ganged like stables for easy conversion to higher and better uses (work or social) once autonomous vehicles displace the need for a garage in every home. Housing developed around *interdependence* (even traditional retirement communities assumed independence reflecting suburban patterns) not only keeps seniors out of nursing homes, it also rewards residents for the connections forged with neighbors. A good example of housing fabrics that evolve with resident agency are affinity communities organized around the arts, like the Senior Artists Colonies of EngAGE throughout southern California. Third places centralize venues for work and hobbies as Baby Boomers generally do not view work as an alienating activity.

Unlike co-housing, third place environments are not premised on routinized chore sharing related to meal preparation or child care. Nor is the third place setting a commune, which by definition involves income sharing, usually accompanied by an orthodox lifestyle. Rather, third places host greater levels of improvisation inviting residents to formulate their own terms of sharing and engagement subject to change over time. The pocket neighborhood is more compatible with our objectives given its balance between the autonomous dwelling unit and collective space. Third place ecologies assert more open-ended collectives, supporting boomers' penchant for individual agency. This is why invention within our project occurs at the level of housing fabrics rather than housing typologies.

The Next Economy: Spaces of Hospitality

Cars and homes have lost their monopoly as icons for projecting individual identity, along with the desire to be owned given their carrying costs. Informal sharing economies are recasting the car and home as on-demand components in higher-order mobility and residential ecosystems. Informality has always been a dominant economic force in developing economies. It is equally so now, in advanced economies as coping strategies where ever more exclusive formal sectors are rationing essential services and public goods.

In his book *How to Thrive in the Next Economy: Designing Tomorrow's World Today*, John Thacker reminds us of the latent "commons" quietly operating all around us to close gaps in unmet social needs. Thacker describes an informal care economy for aging, which shifts focus to the "nurture of mutually supportive relationships between people in a real-world context, away from big medical institutions... it's about focusing resources and creativity on the 95 percent of care that happens outside the medical system already, today." Most of this care takes place within the home where "health space" will have to be reimagined "as a social and ecological context, which needs to be stewarded collaboratively in peer-to-peer health." Looping back to where we started with Jacoby's implication that retirement is a collective project, Thacker seconds this with the insight that: "We cannot be healthy alone. . .Health is local and place-based," determined primarily by surrounding social and ecological capital. Such cooperative structures of living recapture value in two sets of stranded assets in aging—the resident and the neighborhood. True smart cities will co-evolve housing fabrics with peer-to-peer networks in an expanded notion of the commons defined as much by hosting people as managing public goods.

Informality proposes an "unconditional hospitality" in a new porosity shaping economy and place. Following his argument on the mutability of privacy noted earlier, Maak unpacks the space of hospitality and its paradox per Jacques Derrida's question of whether "hospitality is not an interruption of the self." The existential paradox of dwelling reverses the resident-guest hierarchy where "the guest turns the occupant into someone who can open his house and be 'at himself.'"

> According to this notion, dwelling only becomes possible as a result of knowing about being a guest; the freedom of dwelling would consequently lie in the symbolic acts of hospitality, in abandoning the construction of self in contradistinction to others and giving up private life for a moment.

The turn in dwelling effected by hosting, whether out of unmet needs or the search for connection or purpose, opens up new territories in architecture prompted by new forms of agency. The architectural consequences of our seemingly experimental sharing economies, as Maak suggests, harkens back to traditional building complexes—from farmsteads to hamlets and palaces—that collectively housed kin, acquaintances, and labor; such sharing was the rule for centuries. These building complexes reflected social arrangements driven by an economic discipline fully analogous to our proposed third places.

Over the last four generations, housing has languished as an under-examined source of social solutions. Whether one seeks promise in the model of successful aging or protection from threat in the deficit model, either scenario portends new investments based in cooperation, place, and resilience. Even the wealthy cannot escape impairment, loss of purpose, or social isolation. Boomers now understand that the best way to ensure resilience is to cultivate a robust social network preceding the need for one. The challenge of longevity is a case in point substantiating Maak's appeal for a "new habitology" to answer emergent needs. This critical science begins by deconstructing the political economy of architecture, triangulating the interests of the building industry, finance, and housing forms constructed today. A building industry, which, Maak reminds us, became very profitable from providing cheap houses, and "dreads nothing as much as the question: How else could we dwell?"

The following three essays are starting points for conceptualizing a political economy in this relatively unexplored habitology. Alexis Denton's essay examines new combinations of real estate products and service platforms for aging through a gerontological lens. Thomas Fisher's essay raises the role of the sharing economy in creating the new commons supportive of resilient communities. More than natural disaster, challenges converging around aging will be arguably the most comprehensive tests of community resiliency to emerge. Daniel Friedman's thick description of disability through an end-of-life story in the acclaimed film, *Amour,* is a necessarily existential insight into bodily experiences that attend aging. While our project began as a housing master plan for an aging Midwestern community, it quickly became apparent to us that designers needed a better understanding of the pragmatic and existential issues surrounding aging beyond the mechanics of access. Thus, our plan in the form of a transferable vocabulary for approaching the socio-cultural dimensions of aging.

A Gerontological Framework for New Senior Living Models

Alexis Denton

Although more than 89 percent of the over 65 population prefers to age in their own homes, many seniors will find themselves in a situation where they need additional care and support. Caring for U.S. seniors is a $300 billion industry expected to grow at an average annual rate of six percent through 2018 and beyond as Baby Boomers age. While there has been innovation within the individual senior living models and in the type of services offered, their overall structure and type remain unchanged. Not since the early 1990s, with the advent of Assisted Living, has a new model been developed. The models that remain are outdated, appropriate for only a small percentage of the population, needlessly siloed, driven predominately by healthcare needs instead of lifestyle desires, and too inflexible to adapt to the culture of the generation aging into them.

To develop new models, existing gaps in care and lifestyle must be examined to elicit desired attributes of new models. Gerontology—the study of aging—provides the framework for this critique with subsets of sociology, psychology, physiology, and public policy. The gaps drawn out in this critique, inform the attributes of potential new models that can act as *both* real estate products *and* service platforms.

Defining Real Estate Products vs. Service Platform Models

Current models of Senior Living function either as real estate products or as service platforms. Senior Living models defined as real estate products are purposefully built for the senior population. **They serve the entire continuum of care, from fully independent and active seniors to those that require continuous care for all activities of daily living (ADLs), including everything between these two extremes. As active seniors in these settings age into needing care, they move to different levels of care along the continuum of Assisted Living, Memory Care, or Skilled Nursing. While they may be aging in the overall senior living community, they are not aging in place because they are required to relocate for each level of care.**

While some of these real estate products offer services as healthcare needs rise, at their core they remain real estate products that require a transaction and an asset transfer to move in. Services are then layered on as needs change. Seniors traditionally moved into purposefully built senior living communities for both lifestyle and access to services. However, recent trends show increases in average age and acuity levels at entry because seniors increasingly move in for access to care instead of lifestyle reasons. Changing desires of the Boomer generation are likely to increase this trend of people moving only when care needs make living independently in one's own home impossible.

Conversely, service platforms deliver care and allied services to seniors in their own homes. These community based services can be delivered in any kind of existing housing stock that is not age-segregated or purposefully built, allowing seniors to age in their own homes. Services provided by companies or individuals are delivered within the home, regardless of the type of home environment. Some models are structured as memberships while others are on-demand depending on needs. Services are typically focused on healthcare and ADLs to facilitate aging in place.

A Gerontological Framework for Critiquing Current Models

The current landscape of senior living is complex, governed by resident needs and desires, business practices, regulations, reimbursement, and the contextual economic market. Each type of senior living has benefits and challenges, and each type is worthy of extensive analysis but a lengthy analysis is not the intent here. Rather, gerontological framework is employed to assess services and environmental attributes of new models that may combine real estate products and service platforms. Within the study of gerontology, aging is examined through the lenses of sociology, psychology, physiology, and public policy. Filtering an individual's *environment-fit* onto those topics completes the framework to define caregiving profiles for an aging population.

Perhaps the most robust area of gerontology focuses on the sociological and cultural topics of aging. Socialization has long shown to have a profoundly positive impact on health status as one ages. The larger one's social circle, the less likely they are to suffer from loneliness, helplessness, and boredom. The frailer one gets with age, the smaller their world becomes as interactions with cohorts are reduced through death, decline, and institutionalization. Proximity becomes critical due to lack of literal and implied mobility. Additionally, as their world shrinks, seniors are less likely to be engaged with multiple generations. Purposefully built senior living models provide opportunities for both structured and unstructured social engagement but primarily with one's own cohort and with a new group of people. There is little opportunity for multi-generational interaction or to retain social ties built up over many years. Aging in one's own home typically does not provide opportunity for structured social activities or interaction with new acquaintances.

Retaining one's native cultural identity is also important in old age. Purposefully built senior living models are typically neutral in their cultural characteristics. This privileges the values of the dominant culture without consciously attempting to do so. This can create a cultural mismatch which increases stress on the individual. Service platforms do not have the same cultural challenge as purposefully built senior living because one remains in their own home with control over expression of cultural identity.

The psychology of aging is focused on the health of the brain as one ages. Many age-related diseases and even normal aging adversely affects the brain, directly impacting executive functioning and memory. The changes that most impact successful aging are those that cause dementia. Those over age 85 have nearly a 50 percent chance of developing moderate dementia. Housing options are limited for those with moderate to severe dementia because it typically requires a 24-hour secured care environment modified for the specific needs of cognitive impairments. In a single-family home, caregiving usually falls on the spouse, which statistically impacts their own health status due to the stresses of caregiving. On the other hand, purposefully built memory care communities are small in scale with specialized staff that provide the safety and security lacking in one's own home. The challenges with this model are financial and social. High monthly rates for these communities are out of reach for low and middle income families. Additionally they require separation of the family and their ailing loved one in an unfamiliar setting.

The physiological changes associated with normal aging and those common to age-related diseases define the types of care necessary in senior living models. Residents are likely to have multiple chronic conditions, even those able to live independently. In addition to changes stemming from disease or traumatic health experiences, age-related changes to the senses are normal. Auditory, visual, and tactile abilities affect mobility, making it difficult for an older individual to navigate their environment. Home modifications can mitigate these challenges, but a purposefully designed environment accommodates them in a safe setting with supportive elements integrated into the environment.

The gerontological study of public policy is focused on regulations that govern senior care and the financial accessibility of senior living models. The industry's regulatory environment models has siloed people into active, moderately impaired, and highly impaired categories. People move through these silos as they lose their independence and need more care. The challenge here is that aging is not linear; the level of impairment does not follow a straight line, but instead can be circular, and can change quickly. Current senior living models lack flexibility in allowing for precipitous changes in health status without a move into a different setting.

There are very few senior living options for those with low-to-moderate incomes. The reimbursement structure further siloes the industry because it pushes people into higher levels of care. Medicare only reimburses for skilled nursing; no reimbursement is available for assisted living and memory care. Care in one's own home, independent living, and assisted living are exclusively private pay and can be extremely costly depending on the care provided. Medicaid is available to pay for skilled nursing only when one either spends down their personal assets or no longer can afford the level of required care.

Most senior living models such as Continuing Care Retirement Communities (CCRCs) are entry fee models where the resident deposits a large sum of money upon moving in and pays a monthly service fee. A large percentage of this sum is refundable when the unit is turned over upon moving out or death. This model assumes an entry deposit from the sale of the resident's home with a large amount of equity in their home. This is feasible only for high income seniors.

Gerontological processes occur within one's physical environment. A successful environment optimizes the relationship between an elderly person and their surroundings. Individuals who experience lower competencies are more affected by the environment. The more frail a senior, the lower their competency and ability to adapt to challenges in the environment. The ideal relationship between competency and the environment is dynamic; the environment adjusts as the individual's functional abilities change. The highest possible quality of life is achieved when the individual's abilities match the level of environmental demands.

Real estate platforms tend to have better person-environment fit because they are built specifically for the needs of an aging population and can support higher levels of care. Because service platforms take place in existing environments, modifying them to support changing care needs is difficult and often not done. Common modifications include adding grab bars to bathrooms but are minor and do not fully support higher levels of care.

Toward Attributes of New Models
As the next generation ages into need-based care, the focus must be on developing senior living models that satisfy lifestyle desires in tandem with age-related changes. Service platform models tend to be lacking in environment-fit, ability to care for high acuities, and social engagement opportunities. Real estate products,

on the other hand, are significantly less desirable because people do not want to leave their home, yet they provide the care and social opportunities that are critical to successful aging. Potential new models should combine the two types so that they have the best attributes of both. These new models may take the shape of small scale insertions into existing communities. These smaller scale environments, while purposefully built, could be inserted onto or within existing housing stock. This would minimize segregation of seniors and allow them to stay within existing intergenerational communities for cultural fit.

The future need points to models that can provide continuity of care across the entire continuum of need. Both the environment and the services must be adaptable to a person's changing needs and minimize moving and disruption. They must be affordable to a broader range of income levels widening access to care. They also must be culturally appropriate and customizable enabling diverse populations to find their fit. Social life must be the foundation of new models so that all types of social engagements are offered across multiple generations.

Shared Space and Sharing Economy

Thomas Fisher

For an aging population, the sharing economy has come at just the right time. Not that many older Americans understand that yet, having spent most of their lives in a 20th century economy of mass production and mass distribution that often treated the elderly as a liability rather than an asset. The sharing economy, which has grown rapidly in the 21st century, turns the previous one on its head. **As the economist Arun Sundararajan observes about this new economy, "prior to the Industrial Revolution, a significant percentage of economic activity was peer-to-peer, embedded in community, and intertwined in different ways with social relations ... (and) today's digital technologies seem to be taking us back to familiar sharing behaviors, self-employment, and forms of community-based exchange that existed in the past."** Design plays a key role in this return to an informal, socially mediated, barter-oriented economy. As Sundararajan writes, "Design your world right. If you don't, it will be designed for you."

The Millennial generation, born between the early 1980s and the early 2000s and now the largest demographic group in America, has propelled the sharing economy, using car-sharing services like Uber or Lyft, house-sharing services like Airbnb, and task-oriented services like TaskRabbit. But the sharing economy holds just as much promise for the second largest demographic group in the U.S.: the Baby Boomer generation born between 1946 and 1964. While financial necessity has driven many Millennials to access goods rather than own them, for Baby Boomers—10,000 of whom will reach the age of 65 on average every day until 2030—the sharing economy holds physical and psychological benefits as much as financial ones.

Shared Housing

Look at what the sharing economy means for housing an aging population. Many people share living situations when young, in college dorms, fraternity or sorority houses, or military barracks. But older adults, too, have need for shared housing as their abilities wane or their desire for community increases. This can range from independent living close to other people in walkable districts or pocket neighborhoods, to sharing some facilities in co-housing and cooperative living arrangements, to occupying supportive housing in senior developments and total life-care facilities.

While some of these shared housing solutions have become common, others—like co-housing or pocket neighborhoods—still face building and zoning code obstacles that reflect 20th century assumptions about residential land uses. The irony here is that Baby Boomers grew up in an era in which reductive zoning laws eliminated many of the housing options that existed prior to World War II—the so-called "missing middle" of everything from two- and three-family houses to single-room occupancy hotels. As this generation has aged and as younger generations clamor for a greater range of affordable living options, we will likely see the return of this missing middle, much of it reflective of the sharing-economy trend of people wanting to live in more cooperative and communal ways.

Shared Mobility

That desire for a greater sense of community extends to mobility as well. Although most Baby Boomers grew up needing to drive to get around, driving becomes more difficult and more dangerous with age. The Center for

Disease Control notes that "In 2012, more than 5,560 older adults were killed and more than 214,000 were injured in motor vehicle crashes. This amounts to 15 older adults killed and 586 injured in crashes on average every day...(with) almost 36 million licensed older drivers in 2012, which is a 34 percent increase from 1999."

Car-sharing services like Uber and Lyft can counter that trend by transporting people with greater ease and lower cost than taxicabs in most cities, enabling older adults to have mobility much longer in life with much less risk of injury or accidents. And with the alliance of car-sharing services and autonomous vehicles, safety and mobility will increase even further by eliminating driver error—the cause of most accidents—altogether. Shared autonomous transportation also allows a greater range of options for the elderly, such as vehicles that can accommodate wheelchair-bound people with a fully accessible lift gate that allows a person to get in and out without having to leave the chair.

Shared Land
Such services also have tremendous implications for the use of space. Older adults in America have gotten used to the idea that every house needs a garage and driveway, and that every store needs ample parking spaces within an easy walk. But as car sharing, at least in metropolitan areas, becomes pervasive and less expensive than owning and driving a vehicle, the need to store or park cars will dwindle and with it, the need for most garages, ramps, and parking lots.

The space that this frees up for other uses will give people and communities options that they didn't have before. Attached garages can become accessory dwelling units or in-law suites to accommodate multi-generational living arrangements well suited to grandparents as much their children and grandchildren. Unused garages can also serve as home-offices, craft spaces, or recreational rooms, all useful in keeping an aging population active. Meanwhile, abandoned parking lots can give municipalities space for affordable housing close to shopping and transportation routes or for public parks that have proven physically and psychologically beneficial for those who live near them, young and old alike.

Shared Streets
The coming transportation revolution will have equally dramatic effects on public space. Millennials and Baby Boomers have both gravitated toward denser and more walkable neighborhoods for different reasons. Financial necessity has driven many Millennials in this direction, since urban living allows a person to own less and access public infrastructure more. For Baby Boomers, the desire to live in smaller quarters and in closer proximity to others may come more from the tendency of older people to shed their possessions and simplify their lives.

The increased pedestrian activity of denser, walkable communities will make the design of streets and sidewalks particularly important. Complete streets—in which pedestrians, bikes, cars, buses, and green infrastructure share the same right-of-way—represent one version of a shared public realm. A further development of this will come with shared autonomous vehicles, which require fewer and narrower lanes and allow for much wider sidewalks. That will, in turn, increase the amount of space available for social activities of all sorts: from conversing with friends to simply sitting and watching the world go by. For an aging population vulnerable to injury or isolation, this shared and more secure streetscape bodes well.

Shared Infrastructure
The sharing economy will increase the resilience not only of individuals, but of municipalities as well. Research has shown how municipalities

that have long embraced low-density development and high-cost infrastructure often face a situation in which they have nowhere near enough tax revenue to repair or replace the roads and sewers that they have put in place. The Baby Boom generation that helped fuel "sprawl" has a role to play here. Rather than pass on an enormous infrastructure bill to younger generations, both the young and old need to support efforts to increase density in their communities to ensure that municipalities, in the future, have the revenue needed to pay the infrastructure bill as it comes due.

This shared generational responsibility has other benefits as well. Surveys show a sizable percentage of older people in suburbs do not want to continue to live in low-density "sprawl" and to be dependent on others to get around. While car-sharing services can help reduce that dependence, such services become less efficient the greater the distance people must travel and even unavailable at densities too low to justify the cost. Creating denser developments in suburbs and at the core of smaller towns increases the municipal tax base and uses the existing infrastructure more efficiently. Density can also increase the independence of the elderly and the number of sharing-economy services available to them.

Shared Access
Access to the sharing economy needs to cross socio-economic lines as well as generational ones. While the Millennial and Baby Boom generations share a desire to live more simply and more closely together, the financial situation of people in each generation differs greatly and how those inequities get addressed will determine how much everyone thrives. The political situation in the U.S., as well as in the U.K. and parts of Europe, show a growing populist revolt against economic inequality in which a relatively few prosper and many get left behind. As a result, access to opportunity and employment will likely remain a dominant issue in the decades ahead, even as record numbers of people retire from the workforce.

The sharing economy can make a difference here. By increasing access to goods and services and charging only when resources get used, sharing-economy businesses have helped reduce the financial burden of people with limited means. But the sharing economy has also made it much easier for people of all ages to start businesses by increasing access to investment through crowd-funding and micro-lending sites, to utilize existing resources as a source of revenue such as renting out a spare bedroom through Airbnb, and to offer services in a much more flexible way by letting people determine how many hours they work. For an aging population, this allows people to stay active and earn additional income without working fulltime. And for disadvantaged people of all ages, it enables them to diversify their income streams, to work mostly out of their homes, and to leverage the value of the skills and resources they already have.

Shared Futures
Another aspect of current American politics revolves around the divide between metropolitan regions and rural areas. This divide results, in part, from the globalization of national economies, which have favored urban areas over rural ones and led to a growing gap in income and opportunity between the two. Here too, the sharing economy can play an important role. By its very nature, this economy emphasizes collaboration and cooperation rather than competition and contention, helping urban and rural areas find common ground and see what they share.

The global economy, for example, has largely used rural areas for the production of commodities like cheap food or for the extraction of resources like cheap coal. A sharing economy takes a completely different approach. It looks for unique assets in each community—the human, social, and natural capital that exists there—and helps the people in that place optimize the value of those assets. That might lead one community to leverage some physical asset that might appeal to a particular sub-culture—good slopes for skiers, sheer cliffs for rock climbers, clear streams for anglers—and another community to utilize the skills of its inhabitants to produce goods for a global consumer base or to offer services that can be bartered within the local population. All of this depends upon the creation of third places in communities, places where people can come together, share their ideas and assets, and create new economic activity that takes advantage of one of the assets of globalization: the creation of an instantly accessible and widely available global marketplace for goods produced anywhere in the world.

Shared Communities

Sharing-economy services may also look somewhat different in small towns than they do in large cities. Some businesses that depend upon the personal delivery of services may find it harder to thrive in rural areas, where people live and work much farther apart. And some technologies, like autonomous vehicles, may worsen this condition, as driverless farm equipment that can plow and harvest fields day and night or driverless semitrailers that can cross the country without layovers lead to increased unemployment among farmers and truck drivers.

And yet, small towns and rural communities also have an advantage in the new economy. These communities have a long history of sharing resources and services—from barn raisings to goods swaps to equipment exchanges—among people who know and trust each other, an

essential aspect of the new economy. Small towns might pursue a rural cooperative model, for example, in which communities assess their physical assets and leverage their social networks to share knowledge and resources in ways that benefit everyone. The challenge will come in figuring out how to tap the real wealth that exists in every community, however financially strapped it may be, and how to share that wealth in ways that benefit everyone, something that the elders in a community should help lead.

Ultimately, the communities that will thrive in the coming decades will be those that see the advantages of a sharing economy in meeting the needs of our two largest demographic groups. This will help municipalities, large and small, not only attract younger talent, but also leverage the often untapped asset of older adults who, as we have seen, will benefit as much or even more from the economy that Millennials have done so much to create.

Place in Aging: A Brief Note on Michael Haneke's *Amour*

Daniel Friedman

Physical pain—to invoke what is at this moment its single most familiar attribute—is language destroying.
Elaine Scarry, *The Body in Pain*

Body maintenance is hard work at any age. The aim of this essay is to explore the kind of work aging bodies do in the face of illness, pain, and disability. How do these conditions transform the body's relationship to quotidian environments and their objects? Elaine Scarry brings valuable insight to this question in her magisterial study of war and torture, *The Body in Pain*, which assiduously deconstructs the way pain "makes and unmakes the world." Scarry focuses on extreme conditions—inflicted injuries, protracted pain, and violent death—but her inquiry suggests important questions about an under-examined characteristic of growing old, which is that after 60, aging is *painful*. Common indicators of age—osteoarthritis, stiff joints, falls—all generate pain. As the musculoskeletal system ages, so rises the risk of fall-related injuries. "Falls are the leading cause of fatal and non-fatal injuries for older Americans," according to the National Council on Aging. "Falls threaten seniors' safety and independence and generate enormous economic and personal costs."

Pain, Scarry writes, is inexpressible. "For the person whose pain it is," she argues, "it is 'effortlessly' grasped (that is, even with the most heroic effort it cannot *not* be grasped); while for the person outside the sufferer's body, what is 'effortless' is not grasping it (it is easy to remain wholly unaware of its existence; even with effort, one may remain in doubt about its existence, or may retain the astonishing freedom of denying its existence; and, finally, if with the best effort of sustained attention one successfully apprehends it, the aversiveness of the 'it' one apprehends will only be a shadowy fraction of the actual it)." Scarry equates feeling one's own pain as the locus of certainty, and hearing about the pain of others as the locus of doubt. Pain and communication about pain increasingly influence relations among family members, medical professionals, caregivers, neighbors, and in some cases even strangers, since the origins of the word "hospital" connect it to the words "hotel" and "host," among others "hospice," "hostage", which all spring from the ancient Latin root, *hospes*, meaning "guest," "stranger," and "foreigner."

Wherever we consider the problem of design for aging, we are already also in the sphere of the problem of design for pain. Our efforts to ameliorate its effects through environmental design that accommodates physical and intellectual deterioration belie the "shadowy fraction" of our impermanence. Yet good design makes a difference, as this book demonstrates. UACDC's novel prescriptions for real estate products, designed for aging in place, hold out the promise of a better quality of life for a swelling percentage of our population. **However, the aim of this essay is less about "aging in place" as it is the ways aging alters the symbolic structure and utility of domestic environments and their contents, both objects and other people, especially as the muscles, joints, organs, and mind of the aging body begin to weaken and fail.**

Bodies in pain, whether from injury or illness—likewise aging and failing bodies—experience estrangement from ordinary things by degrees, depending on the severity of their discomfort. At worst, pain "unmakes the world," as Scarry suggests; at best it "externalizes itself into world alteration" through the projection of our sentience onto inanimate surroundings, in the form of artwork or poetry, for example. Obviously, any exchange between the sentient human body and its object-laden environment is directly influenced by strength, balance, mobility, and cognitive acuity. As these faculties diminish, so obviously do the properties of the objects with which they interact—chairs, beds, bathrooms, and eating utensils. Both market forces and federal law compel designers to engage domains of body-centered domestic space and activity that expressly address the aging or disabled body, from OXO kitchen products to the proliferation of building solutions that comply with the 1990 Americans with Disabilities Act. In public and commercial facilities, bathroom fixtures, door handles, and countless other interior and exterior details must be designed and dimensioned to accommodate people with diverse motor, muscular, auditory, and visual capacities.

This essay specifically explores the problem of aging and dying *at home*, also what it is that happens to our idea of "home" in that process (mindful that "home" is the word we use to describe "a residential institution providing care, rest, refuge, accommodation, or treatment," as in "nursing home"). Aging, illness, disability, and dying at home are coextensive themes in Michael Haneke's 2012 film, *Amour*, an end-of-life story about an 80-something French couple, classical music teachers, played by Emmanuelle Riva and Jean-Louis Trintignant. *Amour* is a non-trivial film, based on events in Haneke's life. It earned 106 nominations in 48 different international awards programs, 55 awards total, including the 2012 Oscar for Best Foreign Language Film. Needless to say, *Amour* deserves a long, close-grained reading commensurate with its literary and cinematic achievements. However, this essay takes up its narrative as hermeneutical evidence, an interpretation of the convergence of conditions within and around three characters: Anne Laurent; Georges Laurent, her husband; and their decorous and deeply-lived fourth-floor Parisian apartment, the film's principal *mise en scène*. Although *Amour* involves no explicit relationship between problems of design for aging and corresponding residential innovation, it has much to tell us about the ways the meanings of familiar rooms and objects change when the people they surround suffer the onset of age, illness, and disability.

The film begins where Georges' and Anne's story ends. Haneke stations his camera inside the foyer of the Laurent's fourth floor Parisian apartment, framing the front door as it violently bursts open from the outside. Police, plainclothes detectives, and firefighters enter the apartment quickly but dispassionately, watched by anxious neighbors who we see holding their noses, as Haneke's direction dictates. Likewise, the detective in charge covers his nostrils with his wrist, as Haneke's camera tracks him through the apartment: it is clean, well-kept, spacious and intelligently furnished. The commodious foyer reveals tall ceilings and a tapestry; the living room is lined with books and photographs; framed artwork graces every wall; we pass tasteful lamps with linen shades, and a chess set, bowls of fruit; we see Oriental rugs, side tables, an étagère, and a pristine baby grand piano. The detective hastily opens tall, curtained, casement windows, revealing *gard-corps* and a view of the classic Parisian apartment block; he is seeking relief from malodor. The squad pries open the doors to the bedroom, which have been locked and sealed around the edges with tape. We follow the detective into the bedroom past a small, decomposing corpse—old, female, grimly emaciated and clay-gray, dark hollows where eyes once were, yet whose decorum befits the rest of the house. She is clad in a neat black dress, lying in formal repose with her head on a pillow, hands folded over her stomach, a crucifix on her chest, surrounded by brightly colored flower petals.

Haneke cuts sharply and silently from Anne's corpse to his title: white serif letters on a black field in sentence case, *Amour* ["Love"], then just as abruptly, cuts to a theater audience, where we see Anne and Georges, aging but vibrant, sitting in the fourth row, left of middle. Haneke deftly brings Anne and Georges to our attention as they stand to let another member of the audience pass. Anne wears a black sweater over a white blouse, her thick gray hair cut stylishly just above the shoulder with a youthful, fetching part. Even from a distance we can see that she has retained her good looks; she smiles, quietly animated. Georges wears a dark jacket over a dark shirt with an open collar—trim, alert, devotedly attentive. By the look of things, they appear to be in good physical and emotional health, possessing the ease and naturalness one might expect from a couple happily married to one another for sixty years.

Echoing the film's opening scene, Anne and Georges return from the piano recital to discover that someone has unsuccessfully tried to break into their apartment by jimmying the front door's lockset. Unperturbed, they calmly assess the damage and speculate on the motive, meanwhile Haneke follows the couple through their quiet routine—hanging up coats, visiting the bathroom, switching to indoor shoes. In soft, quick strokes, Haneke shows us the effortless familiarity and burnished affection that flow between Anne and Georges, who still flirts with his bride at the door of the bathroom ("Did I mention you looked very pretty tonight?") as she gently comments on her student's performance ("Incredible semiquavers in the presto. Such finesse!"). That night, Georges wakes to discover Anne sitting upright in dark with a blank

expression on her face. "What's wrong," he asks. "Nothing," she relies.

Everything, it turns out, is wrong. The next morning, Anne and Georges sit together in their bathrobes over breakfast at their small kitchen table, reading the paper and quietly discussing their day. Georges phones a contractor about the broken front door. Suddenly, in the middle of their conversation, Anne freezes as though in a seizure, staring expressionless. She is unresponsive to Georges' increasingly impatient appeals. He gets up to dampen a washcloth at the sink, then applies it to the back of Anne's neck, but she is still unresponsive. Haneke shows Georges laboring to walk quickly as he comes to Anne's aid; he is nearly on his last legs, slightly forward leaning, stiff, faintly stooped.

Anne, we soon learn, has suffered a blocked carotid artery. The ensuing surgery fails, leaving her paralyzed on the right side of her body and unable to walk. Her sobering prognosis includes progressive aphasia. The intruder Georges and Anne imagine when they return home from the recital turns out not to be a burglar at all, but another, more pernicious species of thief: catastrophic illness. Trailing behind it, is a caravan of intruders that will slowly rob the Laurents of their dignity and ease: the wheelchair (first manual, then electric); the mechanized hospital bed; the "caregiver"; the diaper.

On her first day back in the apartment after the surgery, Georges helps Anne from the wheelchair into her arm chair in the living room, which tellingly faces his. Anne addresses Georges with determined seriousness.

"Promise me something," she says. "Please, never take me back to the hospital."

"What?" Georges softly replies.

"Will you promise me?"

"Anne…"

"Promise me…"—Georges tries to speak but she cuts him off. "Promise me. Don't speak. Don't explain. Please."

Georges pleads: "What can I say?"

"Nothing," Anne replies. "Say nothing. Okay?"

Haneke devotes most of the film to the couple's wearying attempts to manage this promise, to regularize its inconveniences and somehow integrate them into long-established habits—reading, music, quiet conversation, friends, and visits from Anne's former piano student, their daughter and her husband, all now successful professional musicians. Slowly and steadily the weight of the disease and its disabling effects prevail. Anne's former student (the soloist from the recital), pays a surprise visit, and at her insistence plays the Bagatelle in G Minor; Anne, whose paralyzed right hand gently curls around a handkerchief, puts on a brave face. Later, when the soloist's CD arrives in the mail and Georges eagerly plays it in the stereo, Anne quickly instructs him to turn it off. No more music.

Days pass; Anne steadily deteriorates. One rainy evening, after Georges returns from the funeral of a friend, Anne queries him on the details, and he reluctantly consents—describing a bizarre funeral service—downcast and gloomy in his brown raincoat. Anne listens, then abruptly announces her resignation to her fate.

"There's no reason to go on living," Anne says. "I know it can only get worse. Why must I inflict that on us? On you and me."

"You're inflicting nothing on me," Georges protests entreatingly.

"You don't have to lie, Georges," Anne says firmly.

"Put yourself in my shoes," Georges pleads. "Haven't you ever thought it could happen to me, too?"

"Of course I have. But imagination and reality have little in common."

"It's improving every day," Georges softly pleads, but Anne interrupts him.

"I don't want to go on," she says sternly. "It's touching, all you do to make it bearable. But I don't want to go on. For my sake. Not yours."

Georges resists: "I don't believe you. I know you. You think you're a burden on me. But what if you were in my shoes? What would you do?"

"I've no idea. I don't want to think about what I'd do. I'm tired. I want to go to bed."

Resigned, Georges slowly stands and pushes her wheelchair in the direction of the bedroom.

Anne's stark assessment recalls Scarry's incisive observations about the authority and inexpressibility of pain, which exclusively resides in the body of the sufferer. Anne's pain symbolizes certainty (in this case, of death); Georges, in his denial and incredulity—in his guilt—symbolizes doubt. Although Anne tries to gently guide Georges in his noble but ungainly efforts to lift her from her wheelchair to her armchair, or to the bed, or from the toilet, Haneke captures the inescapable indignities of disability in his unflinching attention to Georges' and Anne's motor limitations and their increasing unease, at one and the same time as he captures their intimacy and trust. Anne's transition from armchair to wheelchair to couch and bed is the system of signs that portend the film's conclusion.

Georges has the pride but not the strength to care for Anne, and she knows it. He struggles to lift her in an out of the wheelchair; he scolds her for trying to stand up on her own, and for falling and breaking the bedroom lamp; he tries vainly to assuage her mortification over a nighttime episode of incontinence that soaks both her and the bed, but the minute he awkwardly shifts her to the electric wheelchair she speeds away from him stone-faced.

She progressively disappears into dementia, refusing Georges' supplications to eat and drink; one night, in frustration, he slaps her. Haneke presents Anne in a state entirely unrecognizable from our first encounter with her at the start of the film. She has lost the faculties of speech and cognition. She moans; she cries "hurt...hurt"; she struggles to converse with Georges and her daughter in rushed, staccato phrases, stumbling unintelligibly through fragments of memory poignantly fueled by her sudden interest in albums of old photographs; finally, all she's able to issue from her failing mind is the word "help" repeated pleadingly. Georges, wearily responding, sits next to Anne and recounts a long childhood story; then after a brief pause, he grabs a pillow from his side of the bed and suffocates her, awkwardly pressing his whole body over her head until she finally stops moving.

Haneke tracks Georges through the delirium of his own despair, as he selects Anne's dress, returns home with flowers, which he prunes at the sink and arranges around her face and body. He seals the doors with tape, transforming his and Anne's bedroom into a tomb. Sinking further into the aftermath of this horrendous act, he hallucinates Anne at the sink, washing dishes. She gently coaxes him into his coat and out the door, presumably with his own end in mind, following hers. This is the last we see of him. Haneke ends the film with a brief, silent shot of the Laurents' middle-aged daughter sitting alone in their living room, which for so long had served as the heart of her parents' world, now engulfed by their absence.

Amour and its critical success arguably reflect the same demographic trends propelling UACDC to take up the question of alternative designs for the aging. A huge and influential American, post-World War II, middle-class demographic now faces the same threshold crossed by Anne and Georges. Would it be going too far to argue that Michael Haneke's Amour is a film about the failure of design? Its power as a story emanates in part from the details of its scenography, and from the unforgettable performances by its skillful octogenarian co-stars, Reva and Trintignant, who show us what happens to a marriage and a home when its spaces and furnishings, however well-lived and burnished by good lives and good fit, suddenly lose all their meaning and value in the face of aging and illness. And yet in its vivid, almost claustrophobic interiority and urban context—the cosmopolitan apartment, the social formalities of Parisian culture, insulation from one's neighbors and one's community—is it unfair to imagine whether or not the promise Anne extracts from Georges (no hospital) would have been necessary had social and spatial systems existed to provide them with a healthier, intermediate alternative, a "third place," in the lexicon of the book that follows. Through thorough research and design analysis, UACDC presents powerful ideas for developments that allow aging residents to thrive in their own communities, among neighbors and strangers, through hospitable spatial and formal innovations that connect people rather than separate them, celebrate their interdependency rather than fear it, strengthen their relationships rather than weaken them. With unblinking specificity, Michael Haneke's Amour delineates the unspoken costs of traditional mid-century urbanism. In contrast, this important work by UACDC demonstrates how good design offers us a much better way to express our love.

Attach Your Home to a Clubhouse and Treat Neighbors Like Family

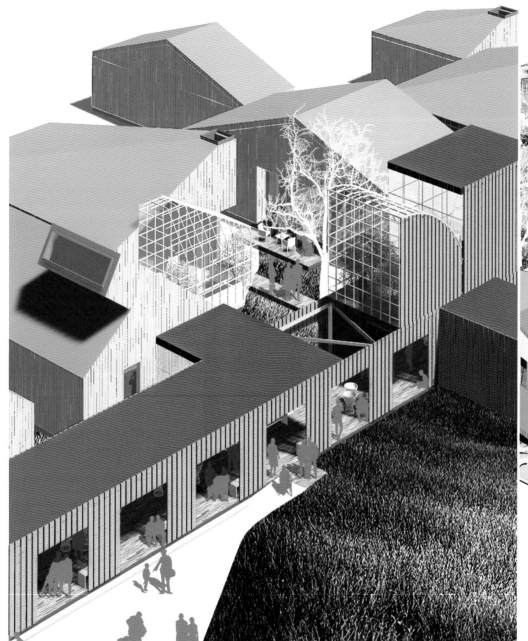

Provide a Work-Hobby Space Connected to the Neighborhood

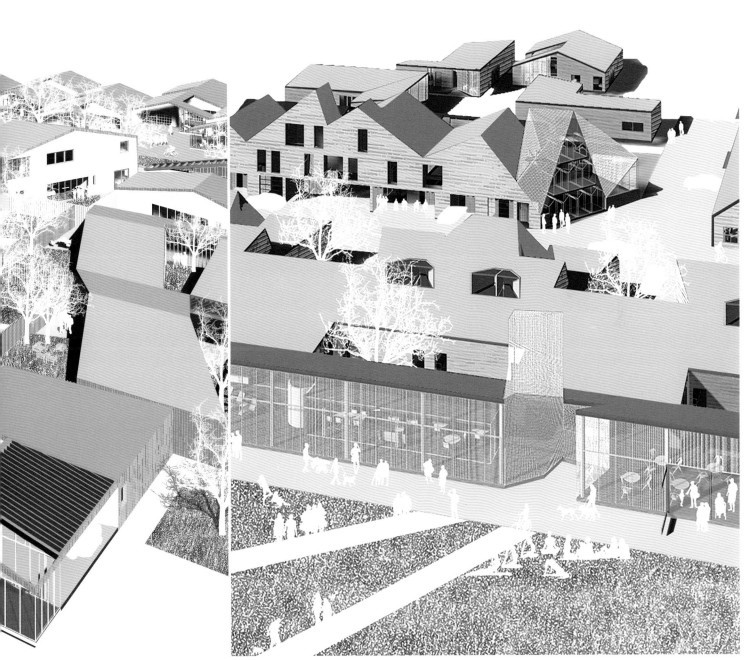

Rethinking Aging and Housing

A majority of residents in senior homes are there due to social deficits rather than medical problems, as friends and family have moved on or their former homes were simply unaccommodating.

The new face of aging embraces the renewal of community and housing density as a spatial fix to accessibility, loneliness, and the search for purpose. The Baby Boomer cohort is a disruptive demographic seeking new dividends from expanded life expectancy. Extended health and robust pensions for some have created an engaged sociodemographic of active, well capitalized and educated 55-75 year olds—the Young-Old—who have rewritten the lifestyle script for retirement. Traditional scripts are dominated by images of the multi-generational home, assisted elderly living, and the utopian retirement community—collectively organized around images of decrepitude and illness, isolation, or leisure. The new face of aging is a call to innovate. *Third Place Ecologies* invents new informal social landscapes among low-density residential development where most will age in place. The proposal is a framework for *aging in community*, facilitating greater inclusivity, vitality, and social connection among neighbors as well as their community—the key to healthy aging.

Aging in place, the default narrative for most, has proven to be equally problematic given its dwelling-centric orientation, which frequently becomes aging alone. Rather, advocates for aging in community observe that a person aging in place, despite being in their own home and seemingly independent, can have a life even more lonely and difficult than that experienced by nursing home residents. They claim that a majority of residents in senior homes are there due

:ial deficits rather than
...cuical problems, as friends
and family have moved on or
their former homes were simply
unaccommodating.

Neither work nor home, *third places* like cafes, coffee shops, bookstores, salons, community gardens, and other hangouts constitute shared spaces of enjoyment and refreshment where informal social connections are formed. Popularized in the book *The Great Good Place*, the third place is essential to creating deep social capital.

Longevity studies corroborate
the necessity of quality social
relationships in healthy aging,
suggesting that solutions for
aging are as much social as they
are medical. Indeed, the city and
higher density facilitate living
alone, given the proximity of
services and greater opportunity
for associations with neighbors
and organizations. Whether rich
or poor, aging presents myriad

porch

lawn/patio

garage

from object...

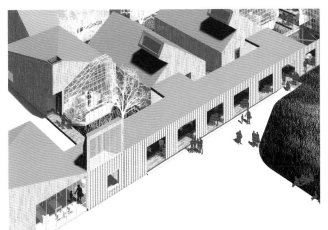

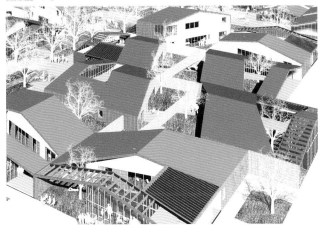

...to third place...   **...to infrastructure**

challenges shared throughout all income classes. Aging in community asks: What then are the urban and housing correlates to this search for purpose and greater connectivity in the post-employment stage of life?

Third Place Ecologies addresses the most familiar site for aging in place: the single-family home in a low-density environment. Yet, elite real estate products have institutionalized our collective visions of aging—the nursing home and the single-purpose retirement community—which house only a combined 10-15 percent of all retirees at any given moment. **Instead, this study explores how the common American residential environment might be gently transformed to support new forms of social and creative activity generated by enterprising Young-Olds.** While the dwelling unit as a discrete place offers much capacity to technically enable healthy aging, neighborhood form suggests a more radical site to examine the role of mutually supportive relationships that underwrite healthy aging and longevity. This is the search for the *third place* and the development of intentional communities through the familiarity of the freestanding American home.

Neither work nor home, third places like cafes, bars, coffee shops, bookstores, salons, community gardens, and other hangouts constitute shared spaces of enjoyment and refreshment where informal social connections are formed. The third place, coined by Ray Oldenburg in his popular book *The Great Good Place*, is essential to creating community vitality and deep social capital missing in most residential environments. As psychologist Christopher Peterson observes: "If you don't go to your third place for a few days or weeks, your return is greeted with interest and enthusiasm. Contrast that with work or home, where your eventual return after days of absence would be greeted with a pink slip or divorce papers."

Despite the American home's gravitation toward ever increasing privatization, there are liminal components like the porch, garage, and lawn whose modulation from discrete object to infrastructural space could transform subdivisions into third places. While *Third Place Ecologies* is studied here through new pocket neighborhood configurations, the process also can be parameterized to retrofit existing suburban subdivisions (refer to final chapter) for the large majority who cannot relocate to other housing. They lack options beyond aging in place in one of the fastest growing housing phenomenon, Naturally Occurring Retirement Communities, or NORCs. *Third Place Ecologies* reworks ordinary single-family housing fabrics through new third place landscapes that revitalize over-regulated neighborhood environments. Aging in community improves upon aging in place to emphasize mutually supportive relationships within homesteading processes.

Care Grids

Third place landscapes are the best prospect for engendering new ecosystems of cooperation in both new and existing residential environments like NORCs. The nature of such place-based cooperation is entirely context sensitive and dependent upon neighbors' ability or desire to organize. Cooperative development ranges widely in motivation, from the need for novelty and creativity to financial and health security. New social landscapes may arise out of emergent informal economies based on post-retirement work, formation of neighborhood social networks, the pooling of caregiving assistance, or combinations of all the above. One need that is surely motivating new structures of cooperation is the expanding demand for long-term care assistance, mostly for non-medical needs. The institutional model of medical care is unprepared for the flood of retiring Baby Boomers. Already, Boomers are building cohousing and pocket neighborhood projects with friends to solve for gaps in the social support and caregiving services no longer available from institutions or as unpaid informal care from family members.

Over the next thirty years, the number of individuals needing long-term care is projected to triple from nine million in 2012 to 27 million. Nursing homes cannot meet current demand nor are they affordable to most given their average out-of-pocket costs topping $80,000 annually if one doesn't carry long-term care insurance. Most future long-term care will take place in the home, displacing costly institutionalized medical care options, especially for social deficiencies. Indeed, the in-home care workforce is the nation's fastest growing employment sector with three million workers employed, and an additional 1.8 million care workers needed in the next decade. Families are playing less of a caregiving role due to a convergence of social forces that have rewritten traditional household structure and familial obligations. Even by 2020, 1.2 million seniors will have no living children, siblings, or spouses, and this number will only balloon.

Accordingly, Ai-Jen Poo, MacArthur Fellow and labor organizer, outlines the case for a nationwide Care Grid to answer one of the greatest social challenges looming in America. In her book, *The Age of Dignity: Preparing for the Elder Boom in a Changing America*, Poo draws parallels with infrastructural inventions in our national history that opened up new public goods like Social Security, the interstate highway system, municipal sanitation, and the transcontinental railroad. Likewise, the Care Grid would function as a coordinated portfolio of federal and local programs in which seniors can age with full care support and services in community. Central to the Care Grid is home-and-community-based care buttressed by greater levels of preventative services, professionalization of care sector work, paid family leave, and stabilization of Social Security. Poo highlights the role of existing neighborhoods and their transformations to provide cooperative care services that allow residents to age in place. "A NORC with a Supportive Service Program typically offers health care management, education, recreation, and volunteer opportunities. Some also offer adult day care, meals, transportation, home care, legal and financial advice, and home modifications." Suburbia could be retrofitted as a collection of Care Grids reflecting higher orders of purpose and security that support lifestyle transitions.

Architect Deane Simpson reinforces this pioneering quality brought on by the longevity revolution. Though he specifically chronicles the rise of the themed retirement community as a specialized leisure product common in Florida, California, and Arizona, Deane makes a salient point generally applicable to many seniors looking to liberate themselves from old age.

> ...the Third Age as a group has sought after and produced new environments that support individual freedom and self-fulfillment, as well as new forms of collective living that unexpectedly expand upon some utopian experiments of the 1960s and 1970s. It is possible then to embrace the Third Age as a demographic group engaged in taking considerable risks to define alternate forms of life, and new environments in which to live.

There remains unexplored ways in which the ordinary American housing environment can support and encourage generativity in the Young-Olds, to address what Gloria Steinem calls an "incomplete social map" that makes senior years an unknown territory.

Why Aging? Why so Disruptive?

"....the values of youth are about possession, consumption, expression and individuality, the values that underpin dignity in age and death are about relationships, connectedness, sharing, and participation—far more powerful drivers for social change."

Charles Leadbeater quoted in *The Big Shift: Navigating the New Stage Beyond Midlife*, Marc Freedman

New cooperative structures of living represent the substitution of community-based resilience for traditional institutional structures, now diminished in their effectiveness. Supports and services for aging have not kept pace with the new challenges in scale. We are witnessing the explosive rise in single-person households, general weakness in affording retirement, diminished access to professional models of care, and a national housing stock ill-equipped to serve residents' changing social and physical needs. *Third Place Ecologies* is resilient thinking, if we take resilience to be the ability to sustain functioning—or better yet, to grow stronger—in the face of disruption and shocks to systems.

Longevity's Changing Household Structure

Every economic and policy sector will be dramatically impacted by the doubling of the senior population as they become 20 percent of the population. Most senior households will be single-person and/or moderate-to-low-income, requiring community-based support to maintain livability within low-cost aging in place. Community, then, becomes a necessity.

One in seven persons today are age 65 or older, by 2030 it will be one in five persons.

One-third of seniors in their 60s live in single-person households, compared to 40 percent in their 70s, and 60 percent in their 80s.

Only 14 percent of growth in residential households between 2010 and 2030 will have children living in them.

Individuals aged 75-84 was 13.1 million in 2010, expected to reach 30.1 million by 2040. Individuals age 85+ in 2010 amounted to 5.5 million, expected to reach nineteen million by 2040.

According to Eric Klinenberg in *Going Solo*, Americans will spend more of their adult life unmarried than married, and will live alone for much of that time.

Affording Retirement

Malthus was wrong according to business author Patrick Cox; the real demographic bomb will not be driven by food shortages, but rather by debt associated with lack of individual savings and ballooning public sector entitlements. Longevity has become our top public policy challenge, and requires restructuring of current social arrangements and institutions.

If individuals lived three years longer than expected—a future near certainty—aging costs could increase by another 50 percent, while adding nine percent to pension liabilities, according to a 2012 IMF report.

Data indicates that nearly half of all U.S. middle-income workers will be poor in retirement. The current average net worth of a 55-64 year old: $45,447.

Half of **Social Security** recipients rely on an average monthly $1,300 payment for 90 percent of their income according to AARP.

Changes in family structure involving weakened intergenerational relationships (childless couples, divorce, reconstituted families, and estrangement) diminish informal caregiving capacity, placing greater demand on professional care services.

How about the caregiver? Usually a family member, 47 percent will exhaust most, if not all, of their savings in providing care.

Future Shortages in Healthcare

Currently, 75 percent of the nation's long-term care budget is spent on nursing homes, half funded through Medicaid once an individual exhausts their personal assets. The medical model of care does not have the capacity to meet future care demand, nor will informal care, provided through family and friends, keep pace either. One trend is to integrate more non-medical long-term supportive care services and technologies into residential settings.

The number of Americans over age 65 who needed long-term care numbered nine million in 2012. By 2020, twelve million will need long-term care—33 percent more in just eight years.

More than 78 percent of elderly in need of **long-term care** receive it informally from family and friends.

The U.S. faces a shortage of as many as 90,000 doctors (and 90,000-200,000 nurses) by 2025, according to the Association of American Medical Colleges. Over one-third of the 767,000 practicing physicians will likely retire within the next decade.

There are more than 7,500 geriatricians in the U.S., but the nation needs 17,000. Unlike other physicians, geriatricians specialize in the treatment of patients managing multiple chronic conditions.

Trends toward Cooperative Housing

According to surveys, 25 percent of boomers are interested in building a new home to share with friends, including communal living areas and shared outdoor spaces. Motivated by recapturing social connectivity absent in conventional real estate products, these *intentional communities* include cohousing, ecovillages, cooperatives, and pocket neighborhoods.

The number of cohousing communities in the U.S. has grown to 162 in 2016, up from 16 communities in 1995, with another 127 in the planning stages. Cohousing clusters dwelling units around shared facilities encouraging spontaneous socializing and collective dining.

Forty percent of all American households want attached residential options in compact neighborhoods with vital streets.

By 2030 new and replaced residential units will number more than thirty million—one-quarter of all units existing in 2010.

Only 51 percent of adults are currently married compared to 72 percent in 1960. Based foremost on building relationships, cooperative housing facilitates opportunities for people to deploy

reserves of social capital.

Substitution of Sharing Economies for Ownership

Boomers and millennials equally drive the emergent sharing economy—a market model based on the peer-to-peer exchange of goods and services (e.g., barter, swap, gift giving, time-share, collaborative consumption, etc.). Besides products and services, sharing solutions involve place-based resources like homes and neighborhoods. Sharing optimizes resource efficiency through reuse of surplus capacity, resulting in lower user costs while increasing entrepreneurship and social capital.

Homes and neighborhoods are becoming sharing hubs featuring tool libraries, food swaps, seed banks, car and bicycle sharing, time banks or labor exchanges—nonprofit models based on providing public goods and creating **asset-light lifestyles.**

For-profit models in the sharing economy are structured around independent contractors who set their own work conditions with negligible overhead and start-up/compliance costs—ideal for post-retirement work and income supplementation.

Seniors in Village model networks broker volunteer care support and home services among one another. Studies show positive impact of social networking on longevity, as participating adults decreased risk of institutionalization by half.

The remaining 85 percent of Americans, however, live in suburbs, small towns, and rural environments like Freeman, South Dakota for whom we propose new housing fabrics that triangulate aging, affordability, and low-density lifestyle. ✶

Some fourty-four million people—or roughly 15 percent of the U.S. population—live in urban cores of America's 51 major metropolitan areas. This project, based on single-family prototypes, would not be applicable to them.

We are upon what experts call the "$3 trillion dilemma." The cost of care for the seventy-nine million Baby Boomers retiring over the next 15 years will be $3 trillion more per year than it is now. The longevity dividend has brought unsustainable costs, but solutions involving innovations in public policies, living environments, medical markets, and social institutions will have to be grounded in new ideas about cooperation.

City +Culture

Freeman, South Dakota
population: 1,306

As rural populations in eastern South Dakota consolidate around select communities, those that offer niche educational, medical, or cultural services will be the ones to sustain their population bases. Complementing Freeman's superior attractions, this proposal adds the latest thinking in housing: pocket neighborhood housing for the aging. While the median resident age in South Dakota is 36.6 years, younger than the U.S. average of 37.7 years, Freeman's median age is 49 years according to a 2014 census data. *Third Place Ecologies* celebrates the deep social capital most places desire—the wisdom, experience, and civic activism that aging populations generally bring. While the proposal formulates a planning vocabulary transferable to contexts outside of Freeman, *Third Place Ecologies* tests housing fabric designs across the street from the Freeman Academy and Freeman Prairie Arboretum. Consolidating new investments around the city's cultural district will add yet another chapter to the extraordinary public and cultural life enjoyed throughout Freeman's history.

History

Freeman was homesteaded in the 1870s by German Anabaptist immigrants from Russia and Ukraine seeking religious freedom and escape from military service. The original town site was soon thereafter platted as a classic Western town expressing the one-mile Jefferson Grid. The town was sold to the Chicago, Milwaukee, and St. Paul Railway Company for $1,500. In 1879 the railroad extended a line into the Dakota Territory from Iowa, establishing a station in Freeman. The initial settlement period in the 1880s brought a full range of businesses, including manufacturing and numerous grain elevators serving the surrounding agricultural community. In 1900 the South Dakota Mennonite College was founded, anchoring the south terminus of Main Street opposite the railroad district on the north end—completing an ideal town layout. In 1908 the college's name was changed to Freeman College and continues today as a boarding academy for grades 1-12 combining Anabaptist principles with the performing arts. Anabaptist settlers to America organized themselves as church congregations rather than simply as families. Ever since, church groups have shaped the area's cultural legacies.

Schmeckfest

Considered to be one of South Dakota's premier festivals, the annual event since 1959 features local food, history, and theater traditions of Freeman. The four-day festival held over two consecutive weekends in the spring at the Freeman Academy, celebrates heritage, family, and the rich musical tradition sustained in Freeman. Each evening a community meal consists of traditional dishes from the area's three Mennonite ethnic groups—the Swiss, Low Germans, and Hutters. Schmeckfest, German for "festival of tasting,"... draws more than six thousand participants from across the nation. After each meal a full-stage musical comprised of area actors is performed. Past performances have included *Oklahoma!*, *Seven Brides for Seven Brothers*, *The Hello, Dolly!*, *Music Man*, *Annie*, and *Fiddler on the Roof*. Music was an important part of Freeman College from its beginning. Schmeckfest is rounded out with food and craft demonstrations, and historical presentations and tours.

one
mile
grid

46

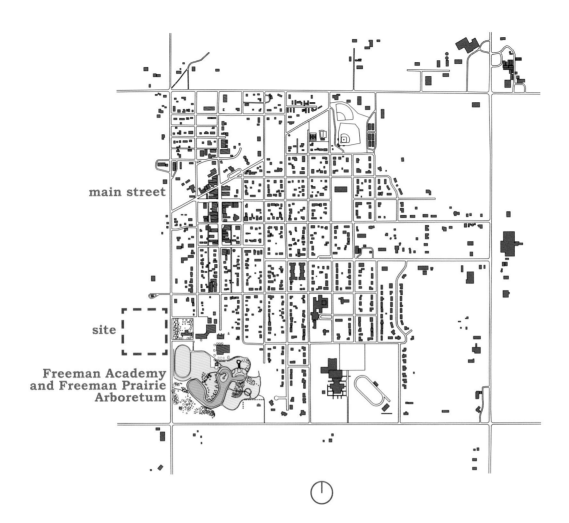

main street

site

**Freeman Academy
and Freeman Prairie
Arboretum**

47

Introducing Third Place Fabrics

From Objects to Infrastructure in Single Story Urbanism

The studio developed three middle-scale housing solutions between that of the house and the total project as "kits-of-parts" or tropes transferable to other contexts. Middle-scale strategies offer the most opportunity for cultivating cooperative lifestyles and intentional communities within familiar single-family residential development. These housing fabrics rework arguably underworked components within residential development—the porch, garage/driveway, greenhouse, lawn, terrace, workshop, and gardenshed—as new neighborhood third places. Third place thinking infuses informality into an otherwise obstinately closed system of development allowing the emergence of social and economic complexity.

The three fabrics are value-added to existing mainstream practices for financing and building the prevailing affordable American home. *Third Place Ecologies* is applicable to the emerging market for accessibility retrofits of existing neighborhoods and homes, keeping in mind that many older neighborhoods have unwittingly become Naturally Occurring Retirement Communities. Thus, the future of care and well-being for the aging will rely equally on environmental solutions rather than solely on medical-based solutions.

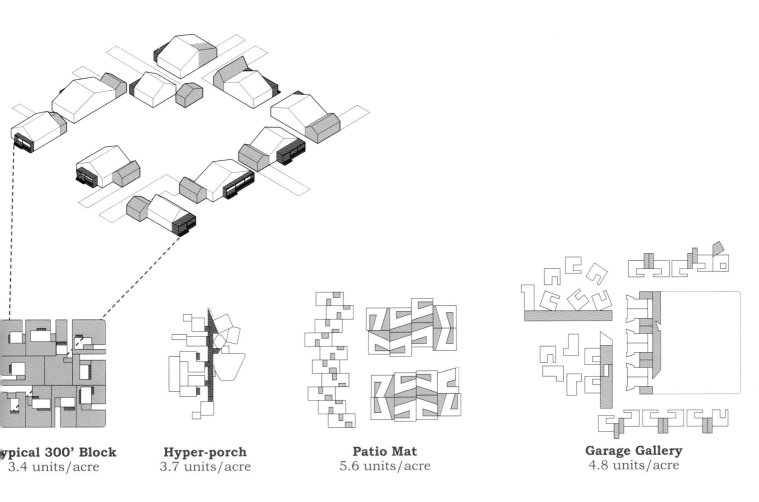

ypical 300' Block
3.4 units/acre

Hyper-porch
3.7 units/acre

Patio Mat
5.6 units/acre

Garage Gallery
4.8 units/acre

Existing between house and neighborhood, *Third Place Ecologies* are an exploration into housing micro-fabrics for new projects, or urban infill, or as suburban retrofit strategies.

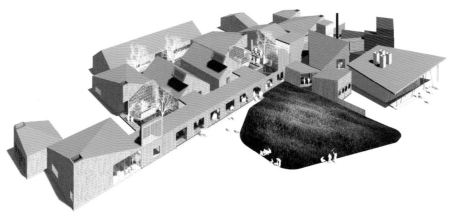

Hyper-porch

Patio Mat

Garage Gallery

Hyper-porch

The porch traditionally, is one of the most recognizable social nodes in a neighborhood. What if we transformed the porch from a discrete object into an infrastructure? Such morphing opens up new territories of social and epicurean experiences akin to that suggested by the veranda, cabana, promenade, gallery, portico, loggia, or a ship's deck.

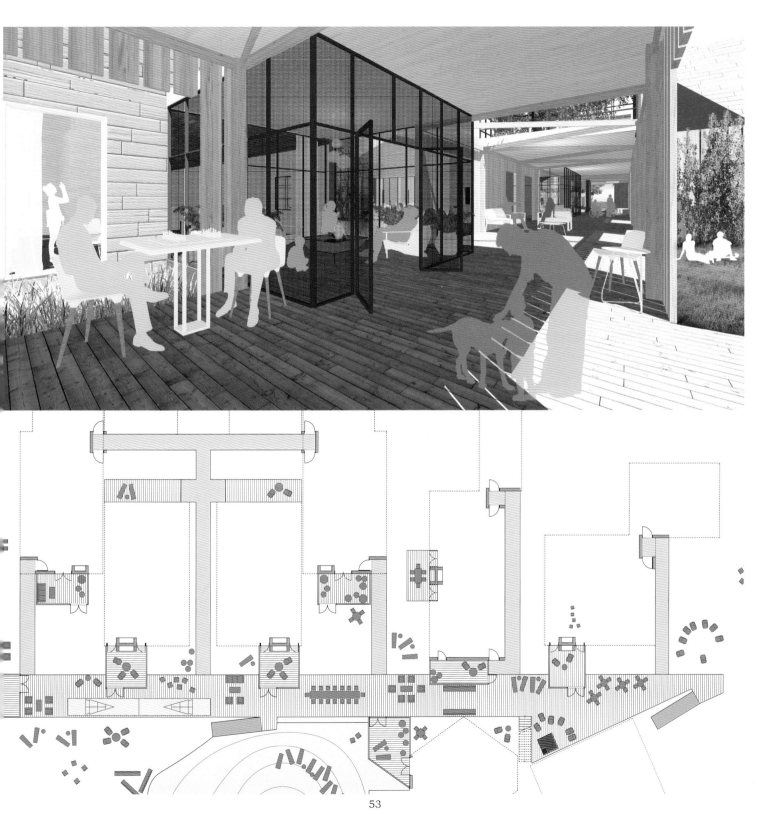

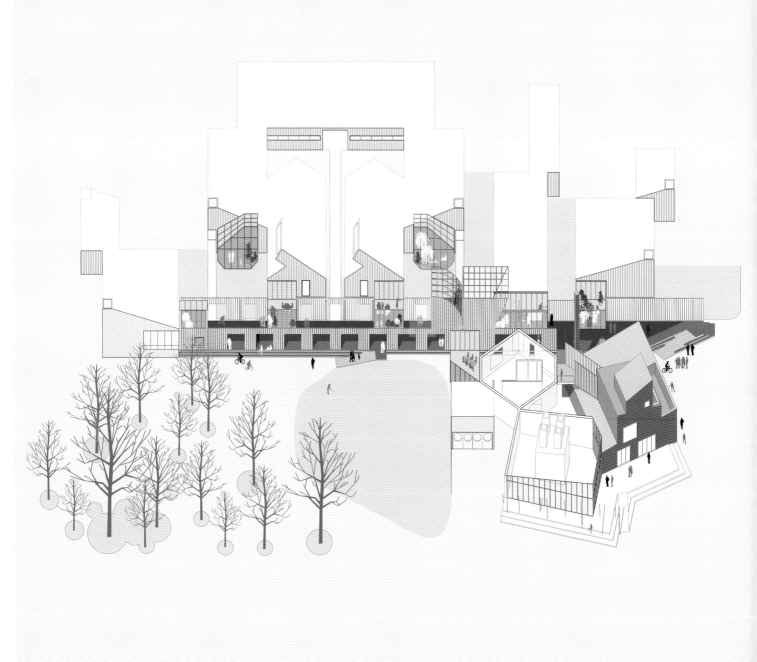

Attach your home to a clubhouse and treat neighbors like family.

Porch as a
social
infrastructure

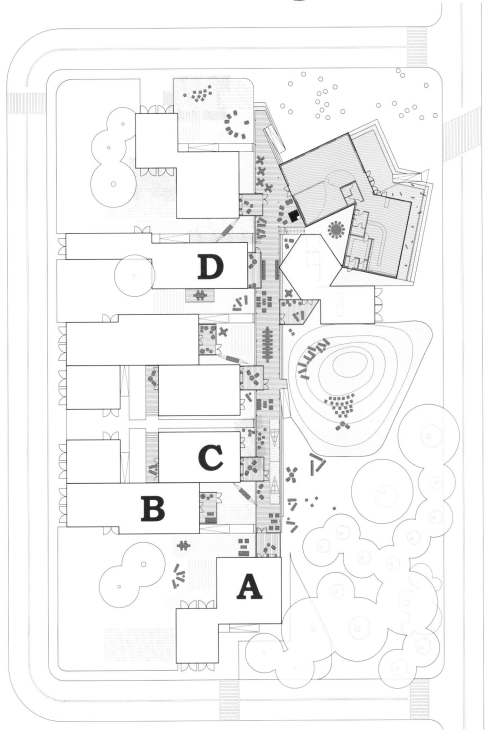

A **four-square**
terminus

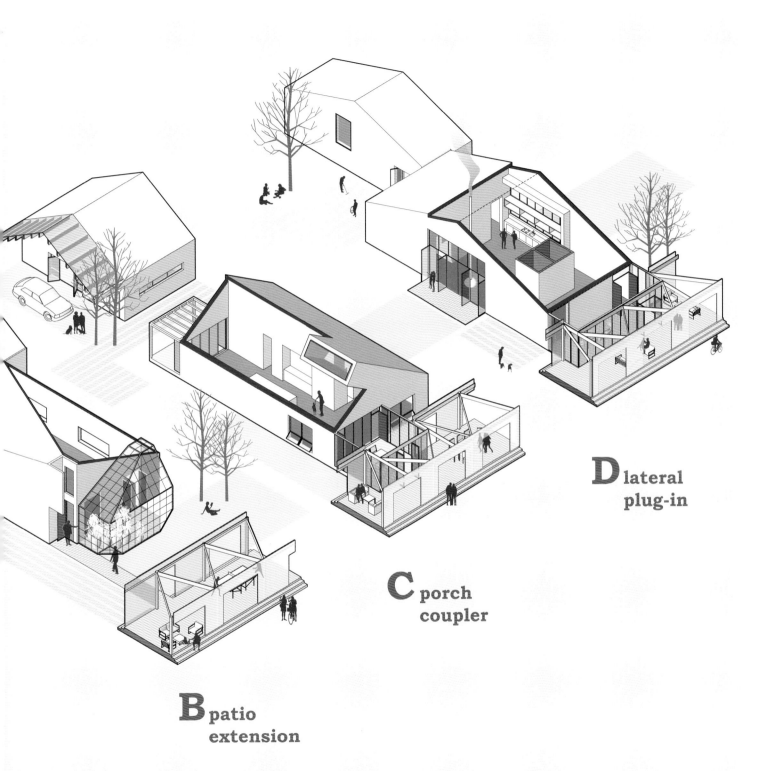

B patio extension

C porch coupler

D lateral plug-in

59

the proximate

the intimate

the public

The explosive growth in aging will motivate exceptional levels of cooperation necessary to thrive in naturally graying communities. New economies of sharing enable neighborhoods to resiliently cope with vulnerabilities generated by greater longevity coupled with coming shortages in healthcare labor. Housing fabrics featuring new kinds of cooperative structures are responsive to the particular needs of aging related to purposefulness,

The Ecosystem of Aging: 21 Principles toward a New Cooperation

access, security, and social connectedness are absent in most low-density development. Thus, *Third Place Ecologies* reinvent low-density subdivisioning to support an interconnected living transect—using what cultural anthropologist Philip Stafford calls the "three circles of life, the *intimate*, the *proximate*, and the *public*." Third places promote porosity among the three realms to create new and recombinant social possibilities toward aging in community.

1

Employ third place as the glue between public and private, residential and non-residential uses, and among different dwelling types.

Like a ship's deck, the third place hosts a variety of uses and settings where no single entity controls the entire arrangement or the conversation. It's accessible and informal, meaning socially managed.

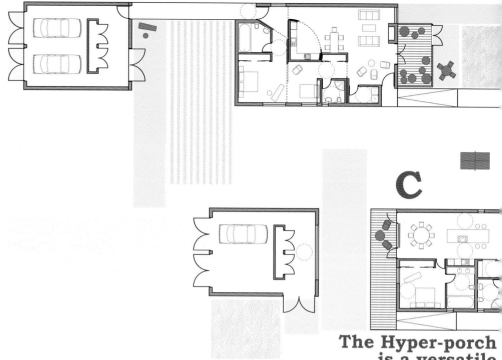

2
Share meals in the third place.

Allocate a third place area for a dining commons to share take-out, pot-luck, or home-cooked meals. Preparation of nourishing meals often diminishes in priority with aging and especially among people who live alone. Sharing food and time can bring new purpose and adventure, while enhancing your social life and health.

The Hyper-porch is a versatile infrastructure, capable of servicing a variety of plug-in components at multiple densities on both sides if desired.

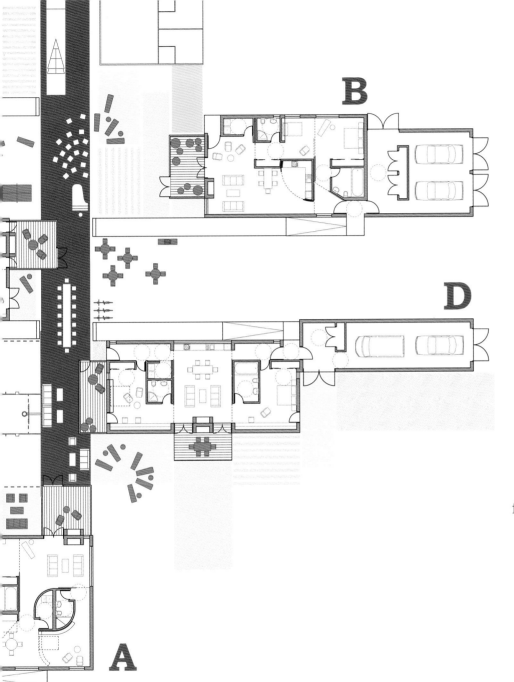

3

Third place fabrics promote efficient sharing of professional home care.

While healthcare for seniors traditionally devolved into a facility-based medical model, future trends point toward demand competition for a limited supply of home caregivers. Third place fabrics integrate real estate models with provisioning of supportive care services.

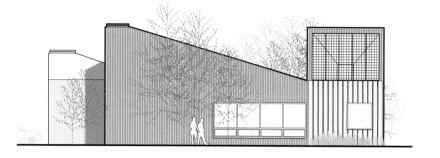

four-square terminus
1500 sqft

porch coupler
1400 sqft

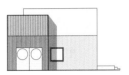

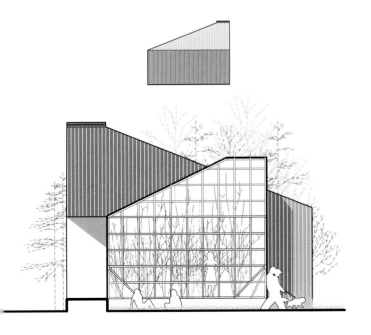

patio extension
1400 sqft

lateral plug-in
1500 sqft

4

Begin with the porch as a street and encourage living rooms to spill onto the street.

The porch also can be winterized as an enclosed lodge linking individual living rooms (intimate), their semi-private porches (proximate), and the collective porch (public)—maintaining the "three circles of life" living transect. Porches motivate regular visits: regulars define third places.

5

Balance privacy with porosity, providing glimpses of the collective.

In a compressed setting, plan housing to allow for easy retreat into the private while facilitating equivalent ease of physical and visual access to third places. People watching people provides a recuperative value—it's their favorite thing to do.

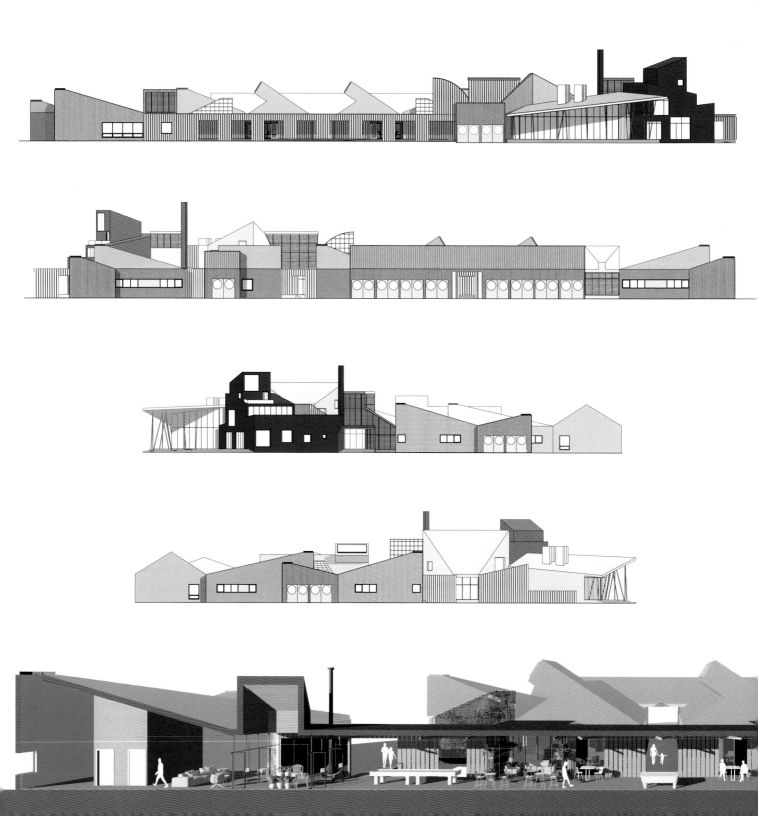

6
Design third places to promote movement.

Movement is healing, and improves balance, strength, and stamina. Most seniors experience two or more chronic diseases, which can be better managed by improved daily routines.

Patio Mat

The patio mat intensifies city and suburb in a compressed landscape where the home's frontage system distinguishes public rooms. How might mat building fabrics deliver a full cross-section of living spaces layering community and privacy? Outdoor living spaces and streetscapes occur at the scale of rooms in an entirely manageable residential landscape. The development can be continually remade through changes in the rooms of residents' frontage systems.

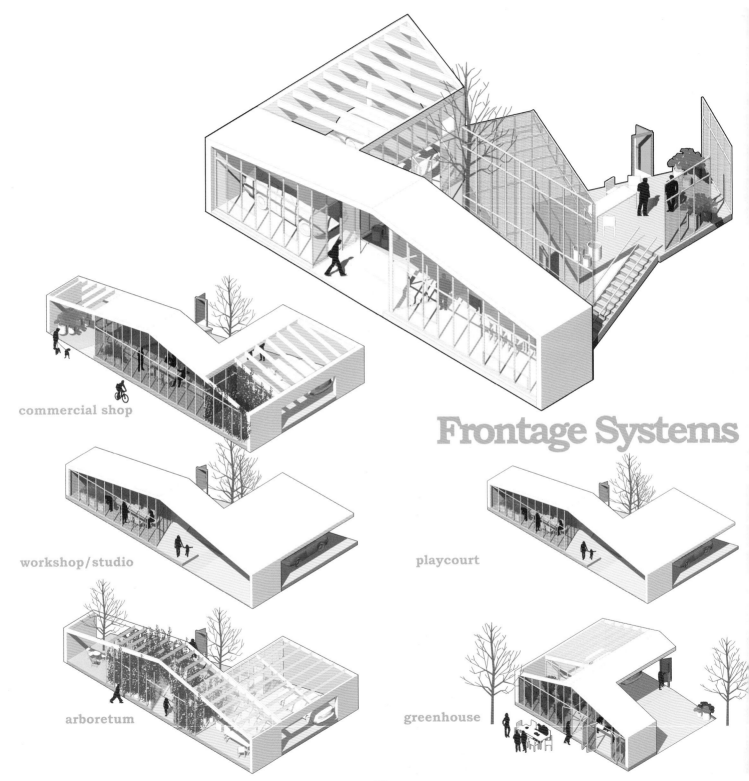

commercial shop

workshop/studio

arboretum

playcourt

greenhouse

Frontage Systems

Create as Many Outdoor Rooms as Indoor Rooms

7

Design streets as rooms that calm traffic where the entire right-of-way is a sidewalk.

Known as shared streets, these streetscapes admit the car but change the street's level of service to privilege the pedestrian, providing healthy environments that reward physical and social activity ... and no more curbs for better accessibility!

Patio Mat as
a system of rooms

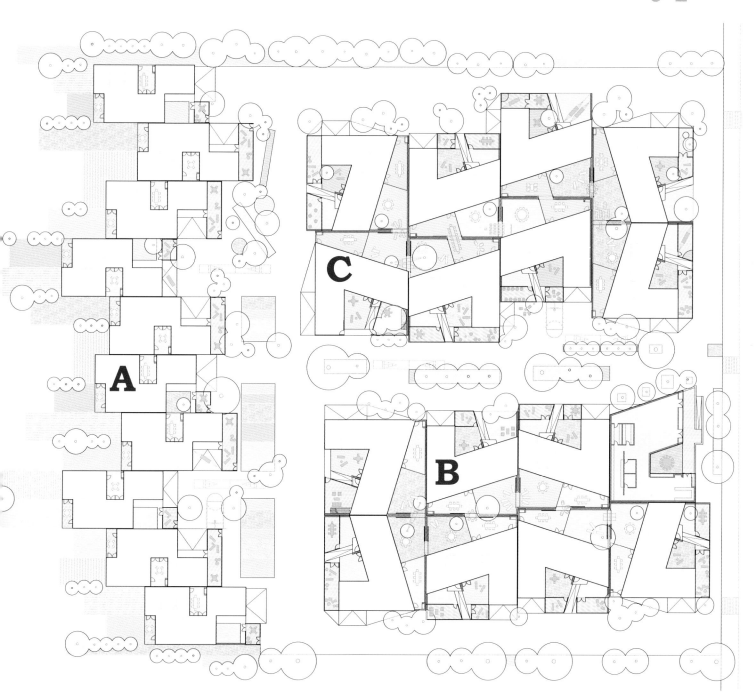

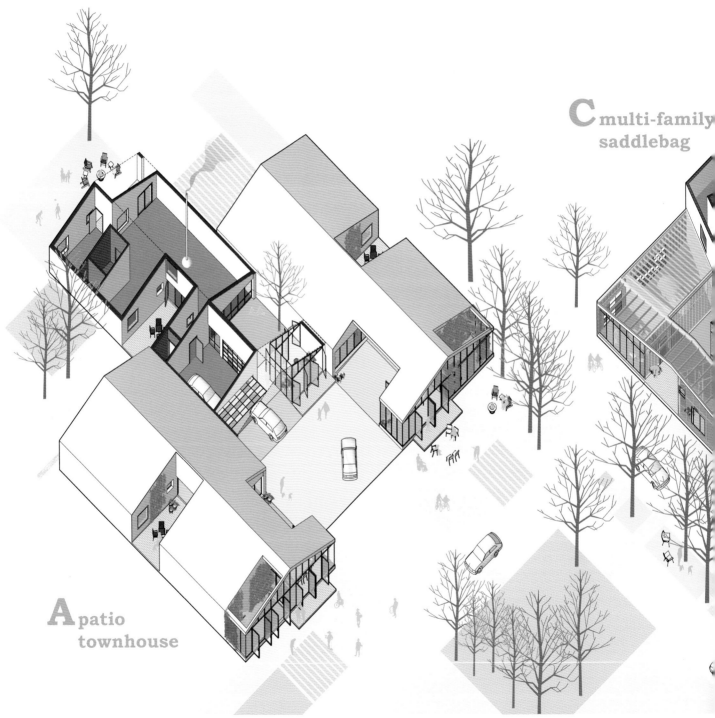

C multi-family
saddlebag

A patio
townhouse

84

B single-family saddlebag

8

In small-lot developments, create frontage systems that house an array of amenities— porches, screened rooms, terraces, carports, garages/ workshops, gyms, and greenhouses.

The shift from the traditional porch as a super-added component to an urban infrastructure of frontage generates informal social and commercial possibilities. These outdoor rooms are one-fourth the price of conditioned space but bring significant returns for the neighborhood while increasing individual privacy.

9

Create a room between the porch and the house, and fill with a garden.

A new spaciousness can be made from layering modest and inexpensive spaces—porch and garden—rather than expanding costly conditioned interior space.

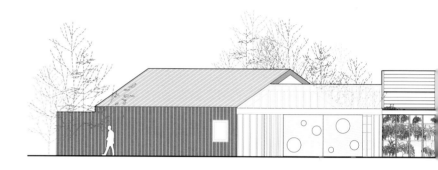

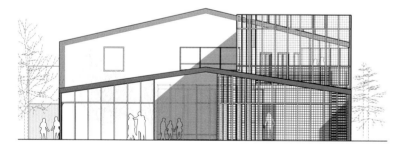

multi-family
saddlebag
1700 sqft
1400 sqft

single-family
saddlebag
1700 sqft

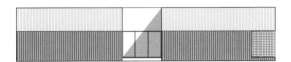

patio townhouse
1500 sqft

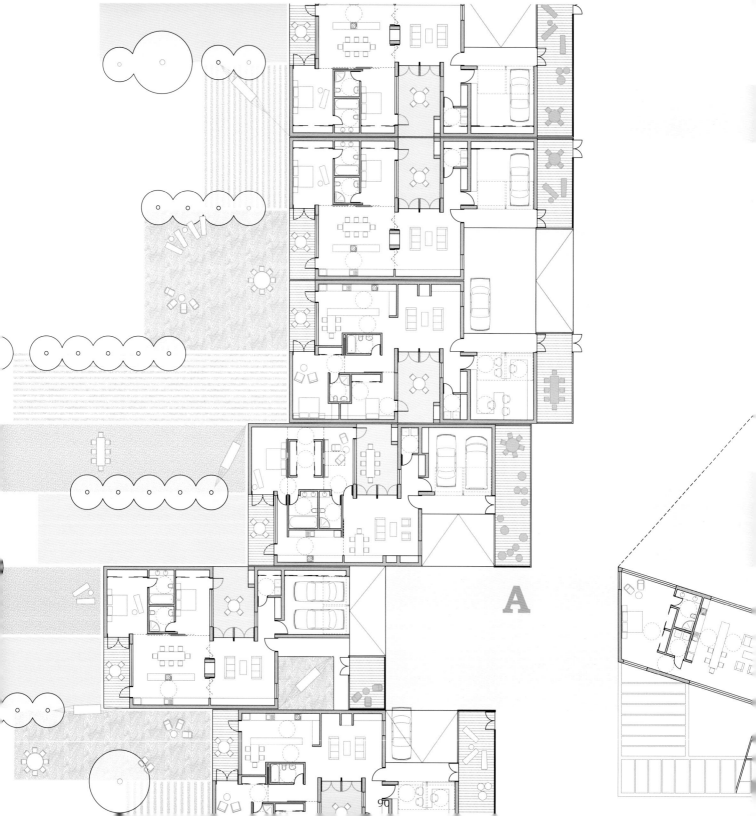

A

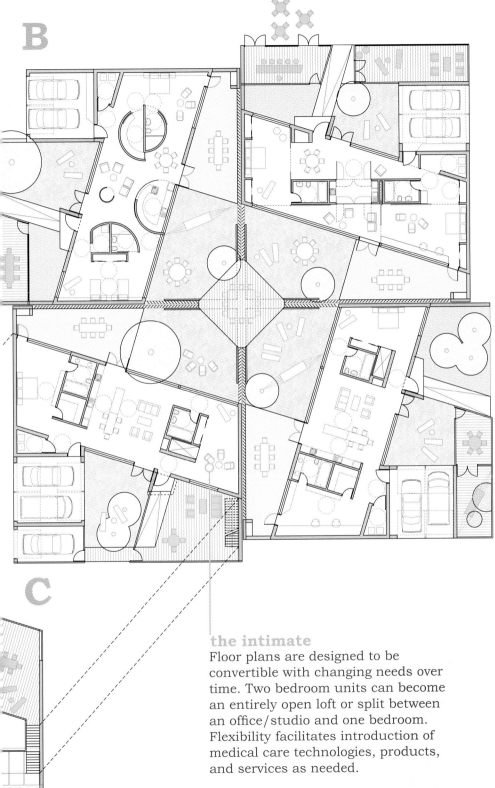

B

C

10

Like in the city, use architecture to frame outdoor spaces. The home is a node in a larger continuum of public and private spaces.

Small-lot developments are premium when they give rise to a purposeful balance between community and privacy—the former often sacrificed for the sake of the latter in conventional suburban development. As aging residents seek community, carefully layer spaces so that one can easily retreat or appear as they wish.

the intimate

Floor plans are designed to be convertible with changing needs over time. Two bedroom units can become an entirely open loft or split between an office/studio and one bedroom. Flexibility facilitates introduction of medical care technologies, products, and services as needed.

11

Gardens can be great third places: move kitchen gardens from the backyard to the front.

Gardening is viral, providing the ultimate social connectivity. Edible landscapes, particularly in public spaces, are a source of fascination for most and the best inspiration for the reluctant gardener.

12
Aim for one-room-deep living areas to allow for windows on both sides.

Two exterior rooms for every major indoor living area is a benchmark of high livability at low expense.

The freestanding porch, splayed from the house, creates a new field condition with novel social landscapes throughout the neighborhood. Independent frontage systems open up opportunities for informal economies and social aggregations nearly impossible in mainstream housing products.

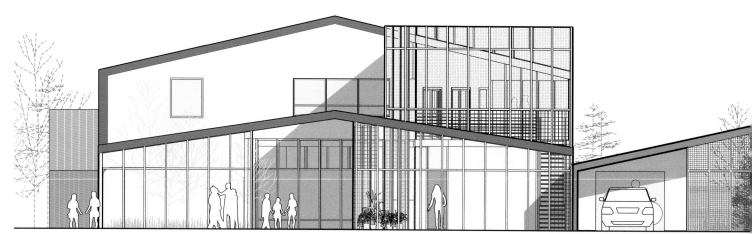

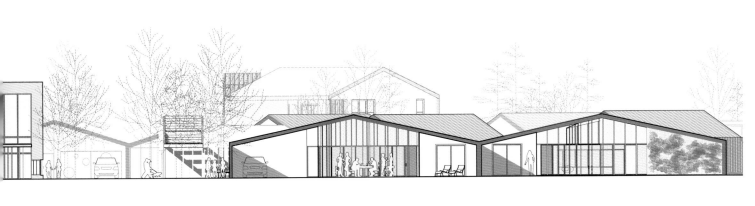

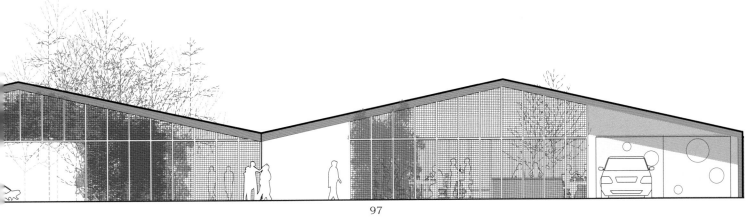

Garage Gallery

Typically treated as a storage facility, the garage was traditionally a work place and the site of other mixed uses including socializing. What if the garage was designed to function as a makerspace; a space for work, learning, performance, or socializing? How might the garage support an extroverted range of activities beyond parking, including pop-up businesses and social events?

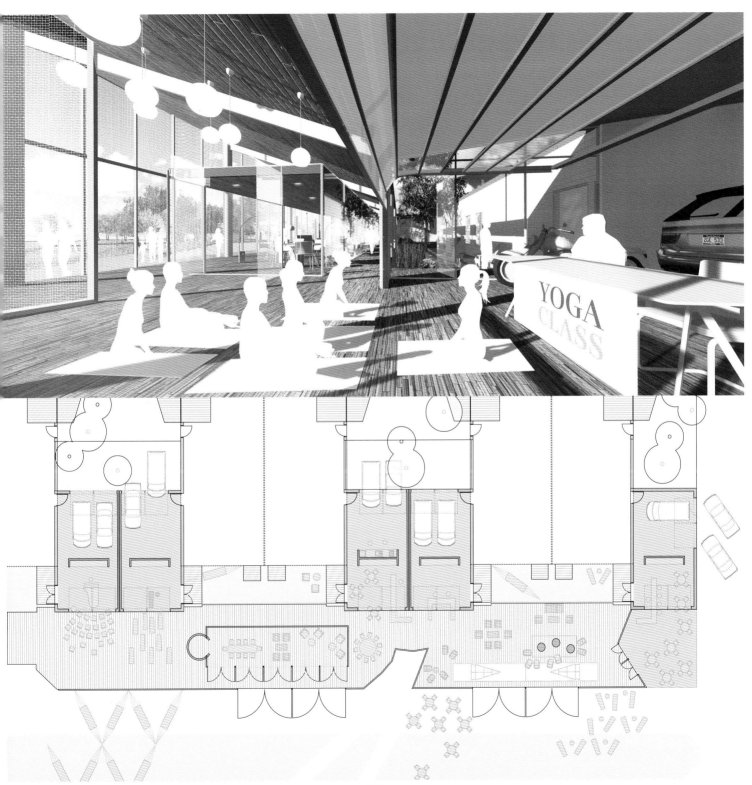

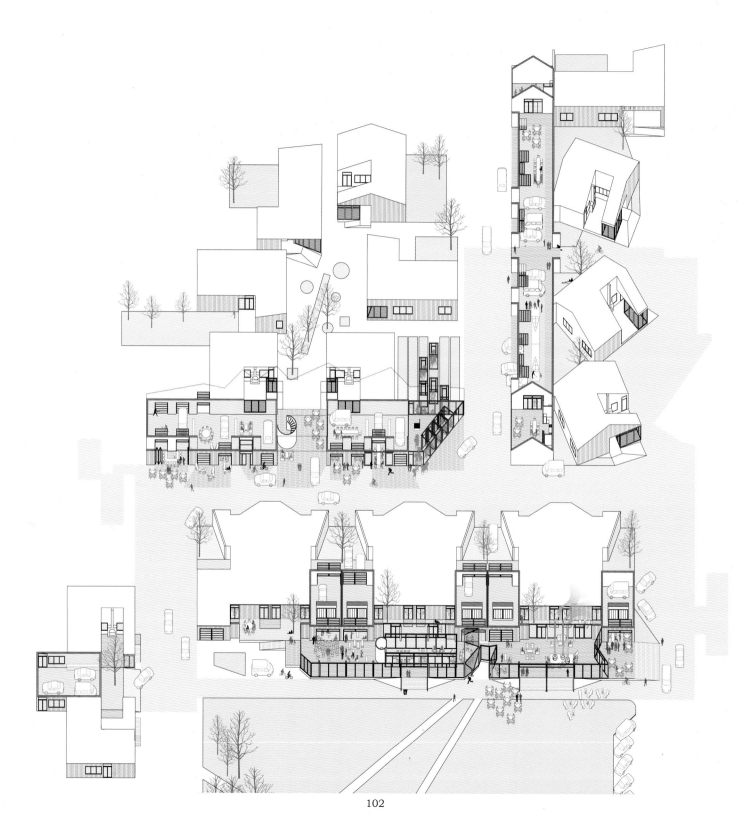

Provide a Work-Hobby Space Connected to the Neighborhood

the public
shared street
/lawn

the proximate
garage/
community room

the intimate
residence

13

Design garage
structures to allow
change of use
over time—from
parking to higher
and better uses like
community rooms,
offices, galleries,
workshops, etc.

The residential garage was
traditionally a smart building
typology that aggregated non-
storage uses like loft apartments
"granny flats", studios,
clubhouses, and ball courts.
Buildings are more sustainable
when designed to accommodate
growing complexity within their
neighborhoods, like when two-
car households become one or
none.

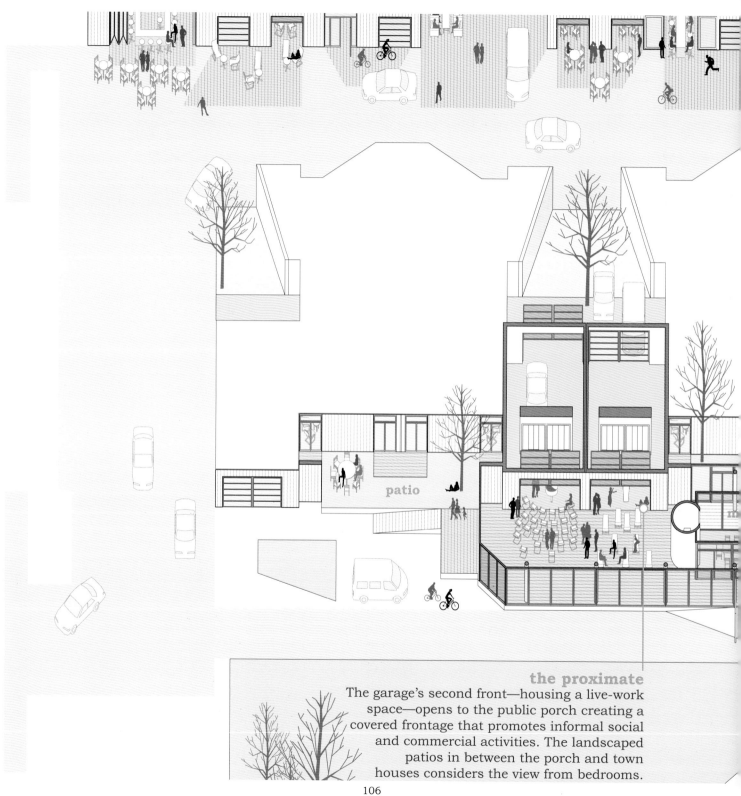

the proximate

The garage's second front—housing a live-work space—opens to the public porch creating a covered frontage that promotes informal social and commercial activities. The landscaped patios in between the porch and town houses considers the view from bedrooms.

patio

the intimate

Garage patio combines entry and porch to home with a modest auto entry from the street. Though modest on one front, the garage's second front sponsors social life within the public porch.

house entry

drooms

bbq area

foyer

terrace

the public

This covered multipurpose public porch hosts a spectrum of community facilities from barbecue areas and open foyers to a glass-enclosed meeting area for formal gatherings. Plug-in live-work garages enhance the mall-like character of this third place.

Garage Gallery as a
spatial framework
to sponsor informal
economy

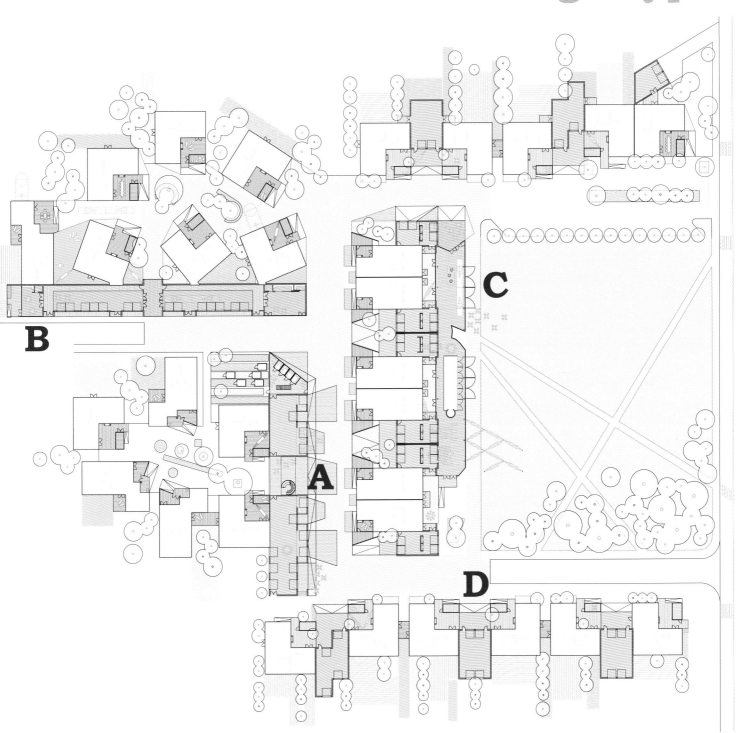

B

A

C

D

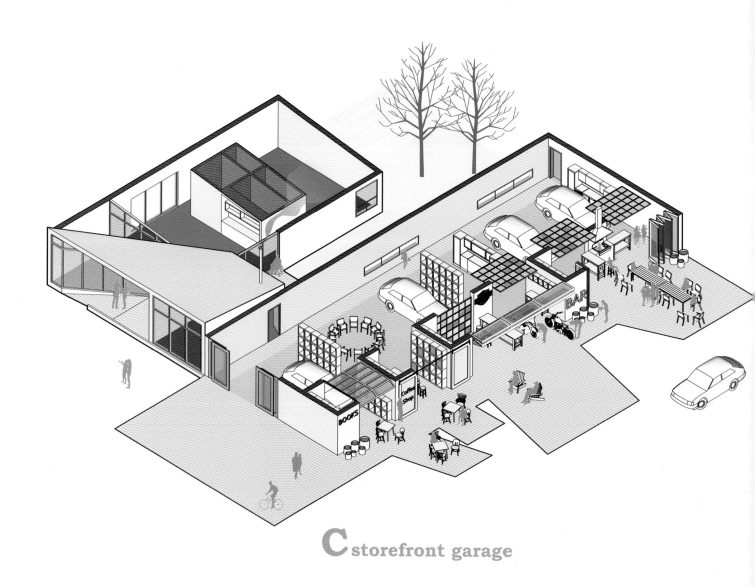

C storefront garage

D garage-porch sandwich

B car lodge

A garage patio

14

Add an extra ten feet to the garage and design the door as a shopfront, allowing pop-up commercial streetscapes.

Garages were always mixed-use spaces and provisional third places in urban neighborhoods. Reset codes to allow informality and spontaneity in these once vital building types. Remember, great third places are ordinary and unpretentious.

15

Begin with the garage rather than the living room as a live-work interface.

What new proximate mix of spaces support encore careers needing a public? Connect the garage with a community facility as another type of live-work interface or space for lifelong learning.

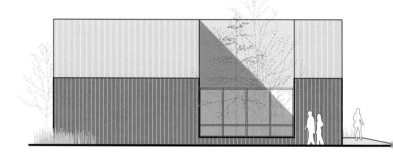

garage patio
1400 sqft

car lodge
1400 sqft

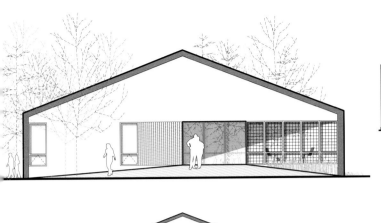

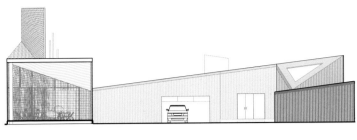

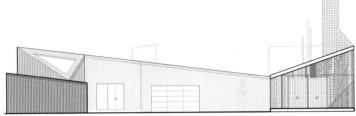

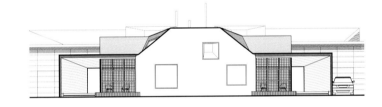

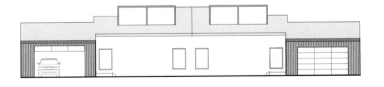

storefront
garage
1400 sqft

garage-porch
sandwich
1600 sqft

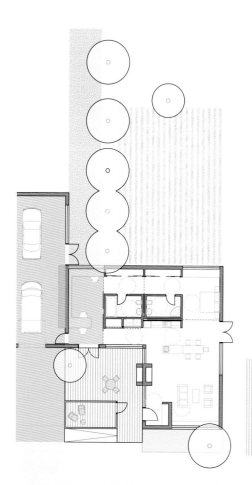

A garage patio

The garage/driveway connects flanking residential patios to create a larger live-work complex, which could evolve to become primarily work when needed.

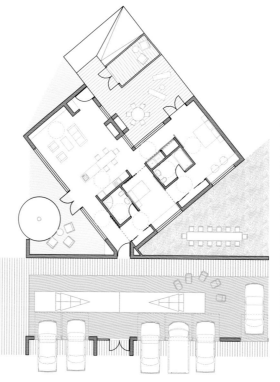

B car lodge

The car lodge is an open barn connected to homes and entirely flexible in accommodating both large and small scale tenant conversions. The lodge can include shared tool libraries and equipment storage, artisanal workshops, community rooms, etc.

C storefront garage

This garage type—where cars park at the rear of the space—allocates valuable street frontage for commercial or social function. The gallery accommodates tenant conversions to higher and better uses than parking with novel storefront strategies.

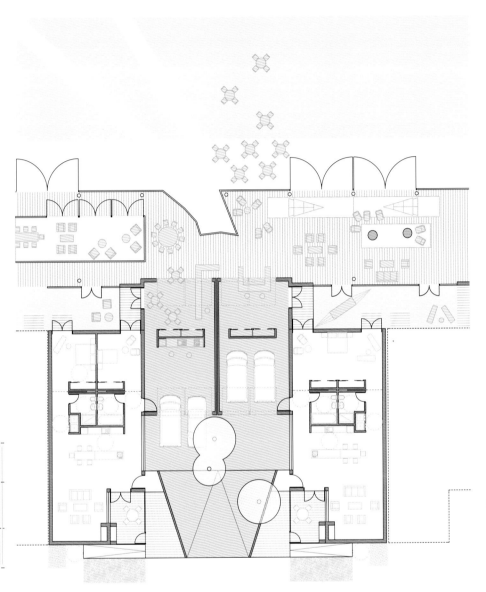

16
From two-car to one-car to zero-car households.

Changes in long-term habits impacted by transportation technologies—i.e., car share and autonomous vehicles—may eliminate future need for the garage as automobile storage. Likewise, ever-increasing participation in the sharing economy and the need for live-work space may require elevating the garage's status from parking to higher and better uses.

D garage-porch sandwich

The garage is a live-work coupler linking home and clubhouse, and serves as a swing space that could favor work and community functions as desired. Mixed-use functions at the garage's pedestrian entry, opposite the auto entry, expand the capacity of the clubhouse.

17

Consider the view from the bedroom.

The probability that a senior will experience some infirmity and an extended stay in their bedroom suggests the importance of views to gardens and a social world for healing and general well-being.

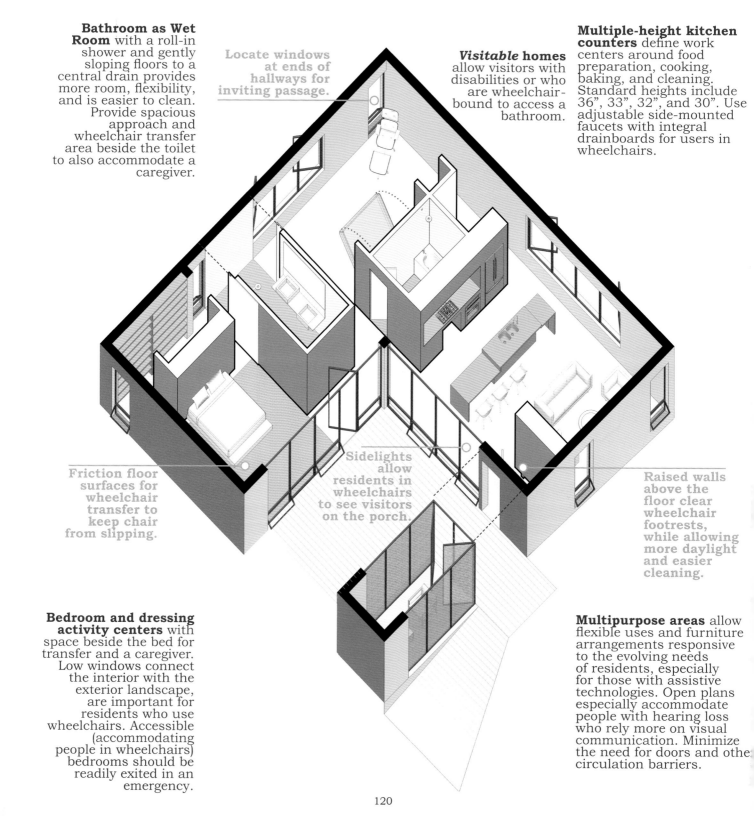

Bathroom as Wet Room with a roll-in shower and gently sloping floors to a central drain provides more room, flexibility, and is easier to clean. Provide spacious approach and wheelchair transfer area beside the toilet to also accommodate a caregiver.

Locate windows at ends of hallways for inviting passage.

Visitable **homes** allow visitors with disabilities or who are wheelchair-bound to access a bathroom.

Multiple-height kitchen counters define work centers around food preparation, cooking, baking, and cleaning. Standard heights include 36", 33", 32", and 30". Use adjustable side-mounted faucets with integral drainboards for users in wheelchairs.

Friction floor surfaces for wheelchair transfer to keep chair from slipping.

Sidelights allow residents in wheelchairs to see visitors on the porch.

Raised walls above the floor clear wheelchair footrests, while allowing more daylight and easier cleaning.

Bedroom and dressing activity centers with space beside the bed for transfer and a caregiver. Low windows connect the interior with the exterior landscape, are important for residents who use wheelchairs. Accessible (accommodating people in wheelchairs) bedrooms should be readily exited in an emergency.

Multipurpose areas allow flexible uses and furniture arrangements responsive to the evolving needs of residents, especially for those with assistive technologies. Open plans especially accommodate people with hearing loss who rely more on visual communication. Minimize the need for doors and other circulation barriers.

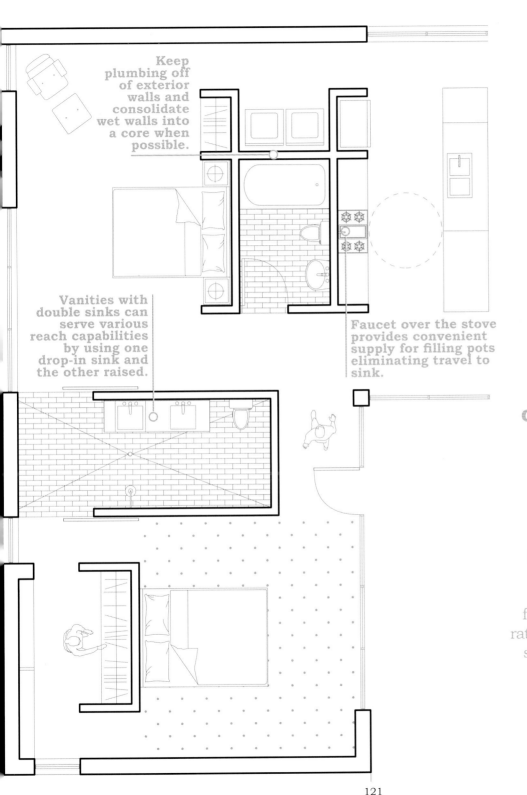

Keep plumbing off of exterior walls and consolidate wet walls into a core when possible.

Vanities with double sinks can serve various reach capabilities by using one drop-in sink and the other raised.

Faucet over the stove provides convenient supply for filling pots eliminating travel to sink.

18

In planning the home layout, begin with a floating core to optimize flexibility and simple customization of floor plans.

Enduring buildings facilitate changes in purpose and use over time—aging in place. Housing fabrics in *Third Place Ecologies* emphasize diversity by readily accommodating functional space modifications rather than over-investing in the signature identity of individual homes.

19

Use the roof as a fifth surface for capturing views and natural light.

Develop interiors as lofts with consideration for how buildings meet the sky. Take care to avoid glare and excessive lighting levels, which become more acute problems with aging.

20

For greater security, arrange porches to face one another in a porch court.

More "eyes on the street" provide collective non-intrusive neighborhood surveillance that signals ownership and subsequent safety, while promoting chance encounters.

tools

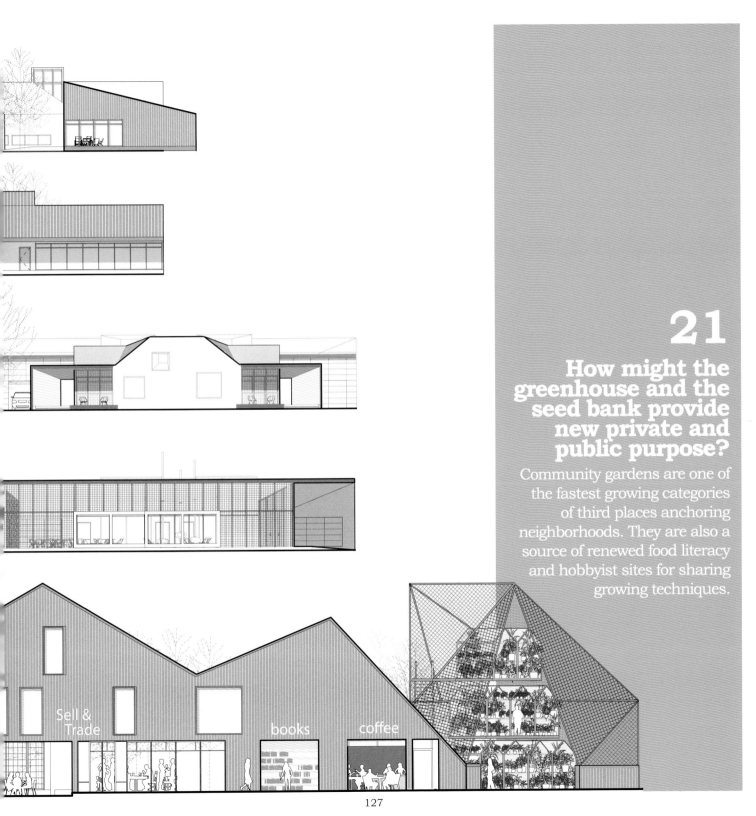

21

How might the greenhouse and the seed bank provide new private and public purpose?

Community gardens are one of the fastest growing categories of third places anchoring neighborhoods. They are also a source of renewed food literacy and hobbyist sites for sharing growing techniques.

Sell & Trade

books   coffee

Retrofitting Existing Fabric

New Care Grids

"First life, then spaces, then buildings—the other way around never works."
Jan Gehl, *Cities for People*

Low-density residential fabrics intrinsically begin with property partitioning and the building; and generally fail to generate civic space and its attendant social life. *Third Place Ecologies* can be parameterized to retrofit existing suburban development for a large majority of seniors who lack options beyond aging in place. Retrofit strategies begin with the neighborhood life and social activities desired, then designate a spatial framework to house these activities—the Hyperporch, Patio Mat, or Garage Gallery—networking existing homes into larger neighborhood fabrics. This can be accomplished through vernacular building without architects, as life depends upon human exchange and energy rather than cultural expressions.

Levittown
NY

Miami
FL

Detroit
MI

Greenhouse

Restaurant

Urban Garden

Pool

Levittown NY

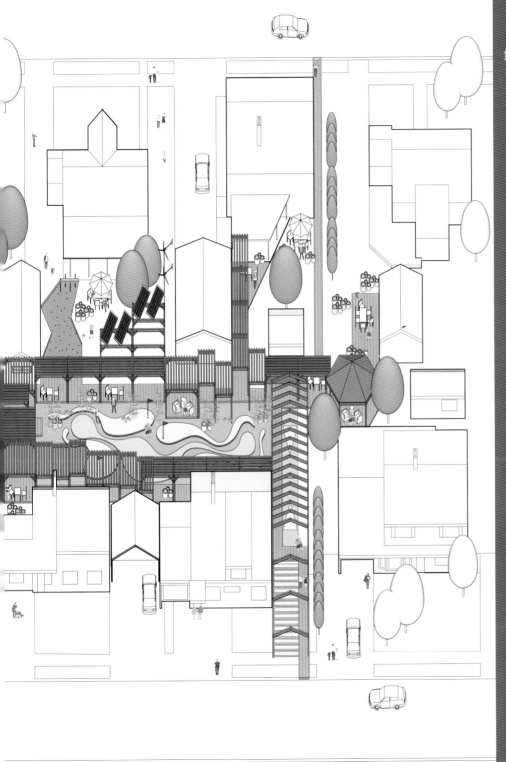

The shared porch can transform zombie residential fabrics that lack demographic and economic regeneration into vibrant communal arrangements. In lieu of individual porches marking house fronts, a hyper-porch in mid-block threads individual homes on both sides of the block to create communal living strategies, or at least establish a shared public realm for greater conviviality. The shared infrastructure can be managed through a Village network, sponsoring

Hyper-porch

a sharing economy where cars, food, tools, labor, and caregiving are exchanged peer-to-peer as collective resources. As an infill hardware, the porch seeds a neighborhood ecosystem welcoming additional supplementary units and plug-in components (patios, screened rooms, grill pits, terraces, gazebos, exercise pools, etc.) as desired by the pocket neighborhood. Much like the deck of a cruise ship, the hyper-porch sponsors a chain of events where there is something for everybody.

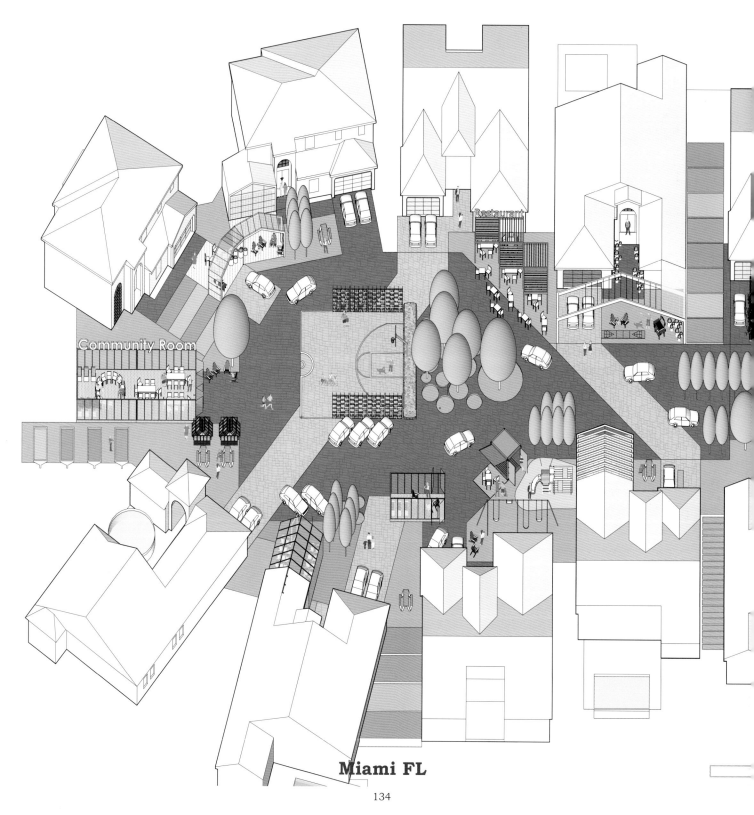

Community Room

Restaurant

Miami FL

Accessible Garden

Community Pool

Cul-de-sacs are a popular suburban street type appreciated for their quietness, but undermine neighborhood connectivity and foreclose the passage of people (life) that connectivity brings. Also called "dead ends," these streets experience very low traffic flows. At approximately $400 per linear foot, they embody a significantly underutilized asphalt investment. A third place retrofit turns the oversized right-of-way

Patio Mat

into a shared space that delivers non-traffic social and ecological services common in great streets. Streets as territories can sponsor community gardens, pavilions and porches, recreational courts, and informal work spaces in constructing new places. Urban mat retrofits servicing large-scale homes, each comfortably accommodating multiple senior households, and can readily enable superior networks for aging in community.

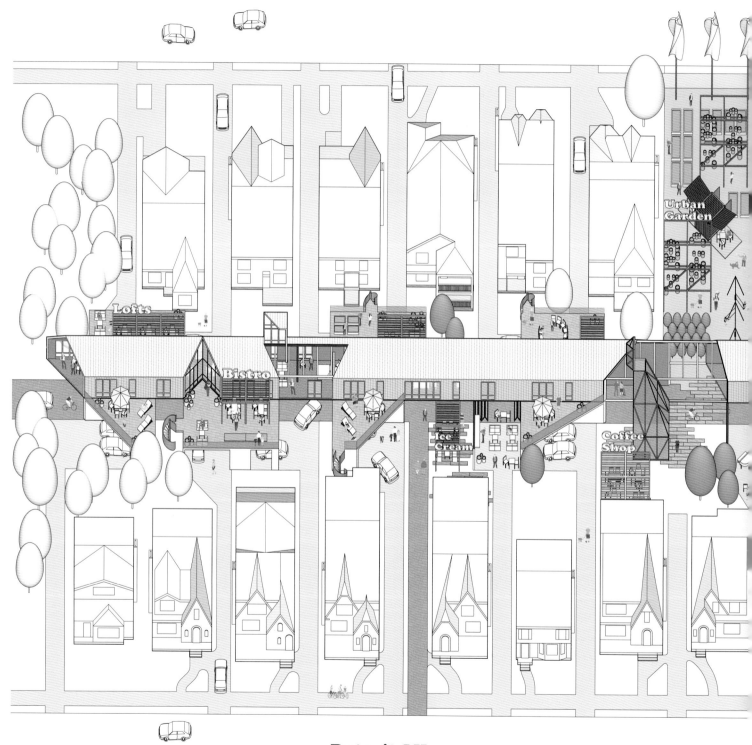

Detroit MI

Thriving neighborhoods begin with the vitality of small-scale spaces on the ground floor. Many "first-ring" suburban neighborhoods (older pre-WWII suburbs close to urban cores and characteristically compact with mixed uses and good infrastructure) are ideal candidates for infill community development that intensifies urban blocks and neighborhoods. Shared garage facilities replace individual dilapidated garage structures with a mall of mixed-use programs—

Garage Gallery

accessory dwelling units (granny flats), decks and porches, senior club houses, covered walking and gaming courses, and co-working and maker spaces. Existing homes can be attached to the garage gallery for extension of living space and connection with neighboring units to optimize communal living possibilities, or at least greater sharing of resources. The gallery structure provides continuity while facilitating varying degrees of individual use and development.

End Notes
and
Image
Credits

End Notes

4 **By 2030, 79 million Baby Boomers will have turned 65 at a rate of 10,000 per day...**D'Vera Cohn and Paul Taylor, "Baby Boomers Approach 65—Glumly," Pew Research Center, 20 December 2010, <http://www.pewsocialtrends.org/2010/12/20/baby-boomers-approach-65-glumly/>

4 **55 percent of households in which the head is over 55...**Joelle Saad-Lessler, Teresa Ghilarducci, and Kate Bahn, "Are U.S. Workers Ready for Retirement?", Schwartz Center for Economic Policy Analysis at the The New School, March 2015, p 2.

5 **Many who now age in place...**For distinctions between aging in place and aging in community see Janice Blanchard, (ed.), *Aging in Community* (Second Journey Publications, 2013).

7 **Studies show that people with strong social relationships...**From a Brigham Young University study cited in: Katherine Harmon, "Social Ties Boost Survival by 50 Percent," *Scientific American*, 28 July 2010, <http://www.scientificamerican.com/article/relationships-boost-survival/>

8 **"A decent life for the old cannot...**Susan Jacoby, *Never Say Die: The Myth and Marketing of the New Old Age* (Pantheon, 2011), p 176.

8 **Notwithstanding this widespread mediatization of retirement...**from a Metlife Mature Market Institute report in Beth Baker, *With a Little Help from Our Friends: Creating Community as We Grow Older* (Vanderbilt University Press, 2014), p 14.

8 **Updated constructions of aging...**for discussion of the "successful aging" model and the "deficit model of aging" see Ashton Applewhite, *The Chair Rocks: A Manifesto Against Ageism* (Networked Books, 2016), p 63.

8 **Nearly sixty-two percent of America's housing stock...**"Housing in America: 2011 American Housing Survey Results", <https://www.huduser.

gov/periodicals/ushmc/fall12/USHMC_3q12_ch1.pdf>

9 **Yet, this household structure will constitute only 14 percent...**Arthur Nelson, *Reshaping Metropolitan America: Development Trends and Opportunities to 2030* (Island Press, 2013), p 5.

9 **The American home was driven...**Niklas Maak, *Living Complex: From Zombie City to the New Communal* (Himer Publishers, 2015), p 160.

9 **Meanwhile, studies show that aging populations fear...**see for example, "Aging in Place in America" Clarity and EAR Foundation, 20 August 2007, <http://www.slideshare.net/clarityproducts/clarity-2007-aginig-in-place-in-america-2836029>

9 **The longevity economy will likely disrupt...** Maak, op. cit., p 166.

9 **Yet, despite urbanists' predictions for a post-recession...**Joel Kotkin, "Don't Bet Against The (Single-Family) House," *Forbes*, 28 February 2012, p 1, <http://www.forbes.com/sites/joelkotkin/2012/02/28/home-depot-lowes-lennarsingle-family-house/#3a8aec05530b>

9 **Through emergent co-housing initiatives...** Jacoby, op. cit., p 83.

9 **Co-housing, pocket neighborhoods...**Daniel Parolek, "Missing Middle Housing: Responding to the Demand for Walkable Urban Living," n.d., <http://missingmiddlehousing.com/dev/wp-content/uploads/2015/04/Missing-Middle-Housing-Responding-to-the-Demand-for-Walkable-Urban-Living-by-Daniel-Parolek.pdf>

10 **Immediate and novel communal forms—"third places"...**The third place concept is introduced by Ray Oldenburg, *The Great Good Place: Cafes, Coffee Shops, Bookstores, Bars, Hair Salons and Other Hangouts at the Heart of Community* (Marlowe & Company, 1999).

10 **Housing developed around interdependence...**Baker, op. cit., p 18.

10 **A good example of housing fabrics...**Ibid., p 112.

11 **In his book...**John Thacker, *How to Thrive in the Next Economy: Designing Tomorrow's World Today* (Thames & Hudson, 2015), pp 127, 134.

11 **Following his argument on the mutability...** Derrida quoted in Maak, op. cit., p 173.

11 **According to this notion, dwelling only..**Ibid., p 175.

11 **The architectural consequences of our seemingly experimental...**Ibid., p 26.

11 **The challenge of longevity is a case...**Ibid., p 25.

12 **A building industry, which...**Ibid., p 26.

13 **Although more than 89 percent of the over 65 population...**Keith Wardrip, AARP Public Policy Institute, 2010, "Strategies to Meet the Housing Needs of Older Adults",<http://assets.aarp.org/rgcenter/ppi/liv-com/i38-strategies.pdf>

13 **Caring for U.S. seniors is a $300 billion industry...**Freedonia, study # 3214, January 2015, <http://www.freedoniagroup.com/Elder-Care-Services.html>

14 **Socialization has long shown to have a profound positive impact...**National Institute on Aging, "Living Long & Well in the 21st Century: Strategic Directions for research on Aging",n.d.,<https://www.nia.nih.gov/about/living-long-well-21st-century-strategic-directions-research-aging/research-suggests-positive>

14 **This privileges the values of the dominant culture...**K. Day and C. Cohen, "The Role of

Culture in Designing Environments for People with Dementia: A Study of Russian Jewish Immigrants," *Environment and Behavior*, 2000: 32(3), pp 361-399.

14 **This can create a cultural mismatch which increases stresses...**E. Kahana, B. Kahana and K. Riley, "Person-environment transactions relevant to control and helplessness in institutional settings" in P. S. Fry (ed.), *Psychological Perspectives of Helplessness and Control in the Elderly* (North-Holland, 1988), pp 121-154.

14 **Those over age 85 have nearly a 50 percent chance...**Alzheimer's Association, "2012 Alzheimer's Disease Facts and Figures",*Alzheimer's & Dementia,* Volume 8, Issue 2, 2012, <https://www.alz.org/downloads/facts_figures_2012.pdf>

14 **High monthly rates for these communities are out of reach...** Alzheimer's Association, "2016 Alzheimer's Disease Facts and Figures", 2016, [video], <http://alz.org/facts/>

15 **A successful environment optimizes the relationship . . .** H. Wahl and G. D. Weisman, "Environmental gerontology at the beginning of the new millennium: Reflections," *The Gerontologist*, 2003: 43(5), pp 616-627.

15 **The highest possible quality of life is achieved...**M.P. Lawton and L. Nahemow, "Ecology and the Aging Process" in C. Eisdorfer and M.P. Lawton (eds.), *The Psychology of Adult Development and Aging* (American Psychological Association, 1973), pp 619-674.

17 **As the economist Arun Sundararajan observes...**Arun Sundararajan, *The Sharing Economy: The End of Employment and the Rise of Crowd-Based Capitalism.* (MIT Press, 2016).

17 **The Millennial generation, born between...** Neil Howe and William Strauss, *Millennials Rising: The Next Great Generation*, (Random House, 2000).

17 **Largest demographic group in**

America... Richard Fry,"Millennials overtake baby Boomers as America's largest generation", 25 April 2016, <http://www.pewresearch.org/fact-tank/2016/04/25/millennials-overtake-baby-boomers/>

17 **10,000 of whom will reach the age of 65...** D'Vera Cohn and Paul Taylor, "Baby Boomers Approach 65-Glumly", 20 December 2010, <http://www.pewsocialtrends.org/2010/12/20/baby-boomers-approach-65-glumly/>

17 **The so-called "missing middle"...***Missing Middle. Responding to the Demand for Walkable Urban Living*, n.d.,<http://missingmiddlehousing.com/>

18 **This amounts to 15 older adults...***Centers for Disease Control and Prevention*, n.d., <http://www.cdc.gov/motorvehiclesafety/older_adult_drivers/>

18 **Car-sharing services like...**Susan A. Shaheen, "Carsharing for Older Populations", January 2011, <http://tsrc.berkeley.edu/sites/default/files/TRB_Carsharing%20for%20Older%20Populations.pdf>

18 **Shared autonomous transportation also...** Tom McParland, "Why Autonomous Cars Could Be The Change Disabled People Need", 3 December 2015, <http://thegarage.jalopnik.com/why-autonomous-cars-could-be-the-change-disabled-people-1688864804>

18 **But as car sharing, at least in metropolitan areas, becomes...**Andy Walker, "Driverless vehicles will free up land to create healthier towns and cities", 21 April 2016, <http://www.infrastructure-intelligence.com/article/apr-2016/driverless-vehicles-will-free-land-create-healthier-towns-and-cities>

18 **For Baby Boomers, the desire to...** Regional Plan Association Report 2016, February 2016, in *Strong Towns*, <http://www.strongtowns.org/journal/2016/2/12/americans-want-walkable-neighborhoods>

18   **Research has shown how municipalities...**
Charles Marohn, "Lafayette," Strong Towns Journal, May 11, 2015, <https://www.strongtowns.org/journal/2015/5/10/lafayette>; "Infrastructure Spending for Dummies," Strong Towns Journal, September 19, 2016, <https://www.strongtowns.org/journal/2016/9/18/more-math>; "The Real Reason your City has No Money," Strong Towns Journal, January 10, 2017. <https://www.strongtowns.org/journal/2017/1/9/the-real-reason-your-city-has-no-money>

19   **This shared generational responsibility...**
Leigh Gallagher, *The End of the Suburbs: Where the American Dream is Moving.* (Penguin, 2013).

20   **Small towns might pursue a...**Caitlin Quigley, "Co-ownership and the Sharing Economy", n.d.,<http://www.geo.coop/story/co-ownership-and-sharing-economy>

21   **Elaine Scarry brings valuable insight to this question...**Scarry, Elaine. *The Body in Pain: The Making and Unmaking of the World* (Oxford University Press,1985).

21   **"Falls are the leading cause...**National Council on Aging, "Fall Prevention Facts", n.d., <https://www.ncoa.org/news/resources-for-reporters/get-the-facts/falls-prevention-facts/>

21   **Since the origins of the word...**Oxford English Dictionary, <http://www.oed.com/view/Entry/88724?rskey=ZbJ4hM&result=1#eid> [accessed March 2, 2017].

28   **A majority of residents in senior homes...**
Meg Miller, "Meet the Architect Who is Radically Rethinking How We Age," FastCo Design, 16 March 2016, <http://www.fastcodesign.com/3058390/meet-the-architect-who-is-radically-rethinking-how-we-age>. See also Matthias Hollwich with Bruce Mau Design, *New Aging: Live smarter now to live better forever* (Penguin Books, 2016).

29   **The baby boomer cohort is a disruptive demographic...**For discussion of this generation's new approaches to aging see Paul Irving, *The Upside of Aging: How Long Life is Changing the World of Health, Work, Innovation, Policy, and Purpose* (John Wiley & Sons, Inc, 2014).

30   **Neither work nor home, third places...**The third place concept is introduced by Ray Oldenburg, *The Great Good Place: Cafes, Coffee Shops, Bookstores, Bars, Hair Salons and Other Hangouts at the Heart of Community* (Marlowe & Company, 1999).

32   **Yet, elite real estate products have...**"A mere 7 percent live in retirement communities" according to Ken Dychtwald, "Two-Thirds of Today's Retirees Say They're Living in the Best Homes of Their Lives: New Study Shatters Stereotypes," *Huffington Post*, 25 February 2015, <http://www.huffingtonpost.com/ken-dychtwald/best-home-of-their-lives_b_6739208.html>. While slightly over 5 percent of the 65+ population occupy nursing homes, congregate care, assisted living, and board-and-care homes according to the U.S. Bureau of the Census, 6 January 2016, <http://nursinghomediaries.com/howmany/>.

32   **As psychologist Christopher Peterson observes...**Christopher Peterson, "Happy Places: Third Places," *Psychology Today*, 1 December 2009, <https://www.psychologytoday.com/blog/the-good-life/200912/happy-places-third-places>.

33   **While *Third Place Ecologies* is studied here through...**For examination of the pocket neighborhood concept as a distinct real estate product see: Ross Chapin, *Pocket Neighborhoods: Creating Small-Scale Community in a Large-Scale World* (The Taunton Press, 2011).

34   **Over the next thirty years...**Ai-Jen Poo, *The Age of Dignity: Preparing for the Elder Boom in a Changing America* (The New Press, 2015), p 3.

34   **Nursing homes cannot meet...**Sara Shelton and Andrea Watts, "Nursing Home Cost", n.d., <http://www.seniorhomes.com/p/nursing-home-cost/, accessed 3 July 2016>.

34 **"A NORC with a Supportive...**Ibid., p 133.

35 **"...the Third Age as a group has sought..."**
Deane Simpson, "Gerotopias" in *Imperfect Health: The Medicalization of Architecture*, Giovanna Borasi and Mirko Zardini, (eds.), (Canadian Centre for Architecture and Lars Muller Publishers, 2012), p 362.

35 **There remains unexplored ways...**Gloria Steinem quoted in Marc Freedman, *The Big Shift: Navigating the New Stage Beyond Midlife*, (Public Affairs, 2011), p 78.

36 **"...the values of youth are about..."** quoted in Freedman, op. cit., p 129.

37 **Every economic and policy sector...**"Housing America's Older Adults—Meeting the Needs of an Aging Population," Joint Center for Housing Studies of Harvard University, 2 September 2014, Key Facts p 1., <http://www.jchs.harvard.edu/sites/jchs. harvard.edu/files/jchs_housing_americas_older_ adults_2014_key_facts.pdf>.

37 **One-third of seniors in their 60s...**Ibid., p 1.

37 **Only 14 percent of growth...**Arthur Nelson, *Reshaping Metropolitan America: Development Trends and Opportunities to 2030* (Island Press, 2013), p 5.

37 **Individuals age 75-84 was 13.1 million...**"Housing America's Older Adults—Meeting the Needs of an Aging Population," op. cit., Key Facts p 1.

37 **According to Eric Klinenberg...**Eric Klinenberg, *Going Solo: The Extraordinary Rise and Surprising Appeal of Living Alone* (Penguin Books, 2013), p 4.

38 **Malthus was wrong...**Patrick Cox, "Malthus Was Wrong: The Real Demographic Crisis Involves Debt, Not Food," *The Daily Reckoning*, 1 May 2012, <http://mobile.businessinsider.com/ catastrophically-

successful-life-extension-2012-4>.

38 **If individuals lived three years longer...**Erik Oppers, Ken Chikada, Frank Eich, Patrick Imam, John Kiff, Michael Kisser, Mauricio Soto, and Tao Sun, "The Financial Impact of Longevity Risk", IMF Working Paper, April 2012, p 2, <http://www.aarp. org/content/dam/aarp/livable-communities/learn/ economic/the-financial-impact-of-longevity-risk- 2012-aarp.pdf>.

38 **Data indicate that nearly...**Amelia Josephson, "Average Retirement Saving: Are You Normal?", 28 February 2017, <https://smartasset.com/retirement/ average-retirement-savings-are-you-normal>.

38 **Half of Social Security recipients...**quoted in William Benson and Nancy Aldrich, "The Aging Middle Class and Public Policy," Blanchard, op. cit., p 177.

38 **How about the caregiver?...**Carol Barbour, "Continuing Care Options: The Next Generation of Care," Blanchard, op. cit., p 155.

39 **Currently, 75 percent of the nation's long-term care budget...**William Thomas and Janice Blanchard, "Moving Beyond Place: Aging in Community," Blanchard, op. cit., p 14.

40 **According to surveys, 25 percent...**Janice Blanchard, "Reweaving the Social Fabric of Our Communities," Blanchard op. cit., p 32.

40 **The number of cohousing communities...**The Cohousing Association of the United States, <http:// www.cohousing.org/directory>.

40 **Forty percent of all households...**Nelson, op. cit., p 44.

40 **By 2030 new and replaced...**Ibid., p 1.

40 **Only 51 percent of...**Blanchard, op. cit., p 28.

41 **Boomers and millennials equally drive the...** "Sharing economy", <https://en.wikipedia.org/wiki/

Sharing_economy> [accessed 28 June 2016]

41 **Homes and neighborhoods are becoming sharing hubs...**For examination of the sharing economy see Gaya Erlandson and Janelle Orsi, "The Sharing Solution," Blanchard, op. cit.

41 **Seniors in Village model...**Candace Baldwin, Judy Willet, Rita Kostiuk, and Natalie Galucia, "A Little Help From Our Friends," Blanchard, op. cit., pp 110-111.

42 **Some 44 million people...**Joel Kotkin, *The Human City: Urbanism for the Rest of Us* (B2 Books, 2016), p 15.

43 **We are upon what experts call...**Citing Bill Thomas, M.D. and author in Chuck Durett, "Musings: Establishing a Healthy, Sustainable Lifestyle for an Aging Generation", The Cohousing Association of the United States, 5 August 2009, <http://www.cohousing.org/node/1708>.

44 **While the median resident age...***City-Data.com,* <http://www.city-data.com/city/Freeman-South-Dakota.html>, [accessed 28 February 2017].

45 **Freeman was homesteaded...**For a history of Freeman, see "The Birth of Freeman", n.d.,<http://freemansd.webs.com/birth-of-freeman>

45 **Considered to be one of South Dakota's...** For a history of Schmeckfest see: "The History of Schmeckfest", April 2017, <http://schmeckfest.com/History.html>.

61 **Thus, *Third Place Ecologies* reinvent low-density...**On the "three circles of life" see Philip Stafford, "Home is a Verb: Designing around the Lifeworld of Elders," American Architectural Foundation, 22 April 2013, <http://www.archfoundation.org/2013/04/home-is-a-verb-designing-around-the-lifeworld-of-elders/>

121 **In planning the home layout...**For best design practices see Deborah Pierce, *The Accessible Home: Designing for All Ages & Abilities* (The Taunton Press, 2012).

130 **"First life, then spaces"...**Jan Gehl, *Cities for People* (Island Press, 2010), p 191.

Image Credits:
7   © Ben Bengston, freemansd.webs.com

31   © Kerrie Kelly Design Lab

37   © Neighborhood Notes

45   © Dick Clarkson, Freeman Courier, © Jeremy Waltner, Freeman Courier, © Ben Bengston, freemansd.webs.com

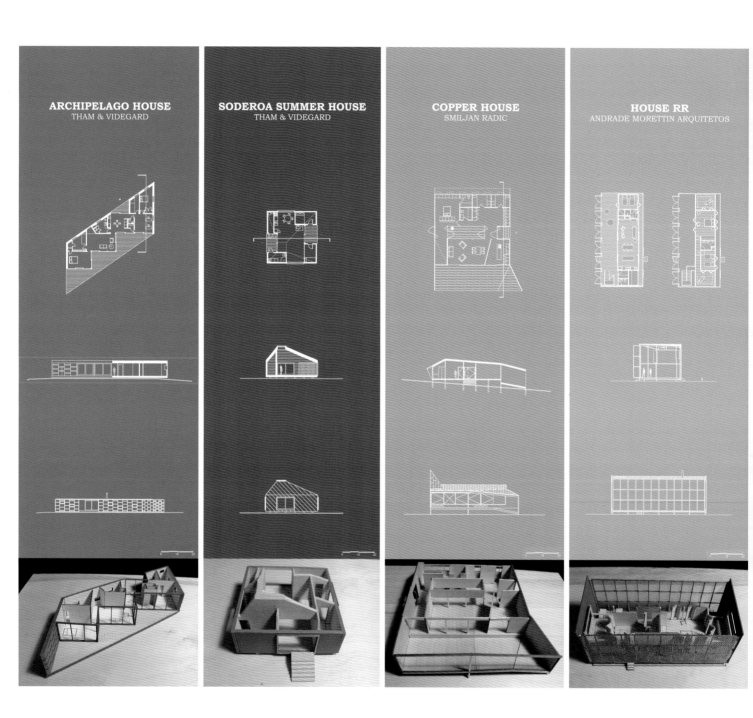

ARCHIPELAGO HOUSE
THAM & VIDEGARD

SODEROA SUMMER HOUSE
THAM & VIDEGARD

COPPER HOUSE
SMILJAN RADIC

HOUSE RR
ANDRADE MORETTIN ARQUITETOS

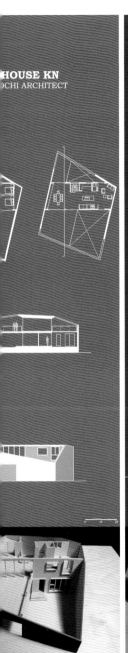

HOUSE KN
OCHI ARCHITECT

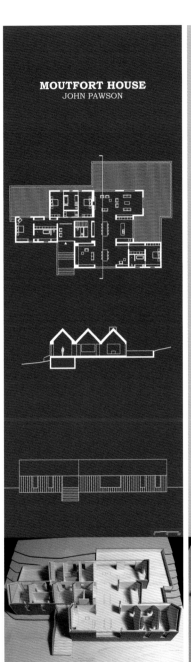

MOUTFORT HOUSE
JOHN PAWSON

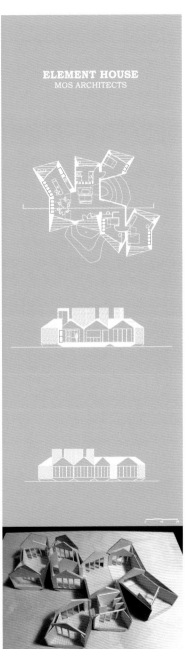

ELEMENT HOUSE
MOS ARCHITECTS

Single-Family House Studies

Precedents in the design of mostly single-volume, modest houses by famous architects demonstrated the **power of typological thinking**. Each type suggested its own condition of framing a complex economy of inside/outside territories beyond a simple collection of rooms.

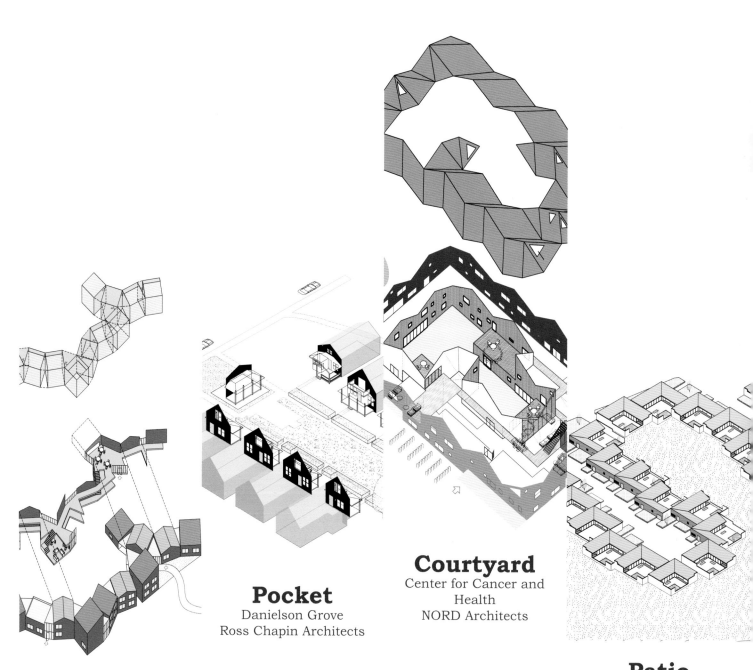

Spine
Home for the Mentally
Handicapped
Sou Fujimoto Architects

Pocket
Danielson Grove
Ross Chapin Architects

Courtyard
Center for Cancer and
Health
NORD Architects

Patio
Fredensborg Houses
Jørn Utzon

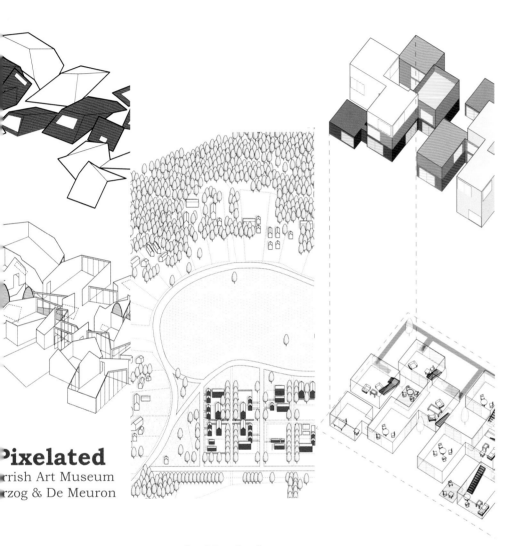

Pixelated
rrish Art Museum
rzog & De Meuron

Subdivision
Jackson Meadows
Coen + Partners

Cluster
Seijo Townhouses
Kajuyo Sejima

Residential Aggregation Studies

Precedents in the reproduction of **cellular components demonstrate wholes larger than their parts**, while providing a thesaurus of formal design approaches. The learning objective established understanding for the typological vocabularies of the detached house countered by logics of aggregation in developing collective housing site plans.

Contributors:

Stephen Luoni is the Director of the University of Arkansas Community Design Center (UACDC) where he is the Steven L. Anderson Chair in Architecture and Urban Studies and a Distinguished Professor of Architecture.

Alexis Denton, an architect and gerontologist, leads the Senior Living practice at the global design firm SmithGroupJJR. A licensed architect in the state of California, she focuses on combining the latest trends and research in Architecture and Gerontology to design meaningful environments and experiences for seniors.

Thomas Fisher is the Dayton Hudson Land Grant Chair in Urban Design and Director of the University of Minnesota Metropolitan Design Center. He was previously the Editorial Director of Progressive Architecture magazine and the Dean of the University of Minnesota's College of Design.

Daniel S. Friedman, Dean of the School of Architecture at the University of Hawaii Manoa, is a Past President of the Association of Collegiate Schools of Architecture, and served as the 2015 Chair of the American Institute of Architects (AIA) National Design and Health Leadership Group.

Project Team:

University of Arkansas Community Design Center
Stephen Luoni, Director
Paco Mejias Villatoro, Project Architect and Assoc. Prof.
Tanzil Shafique, Project Designer
David Marroquin Juarez, Project Designer
Jonathan Alexander Martinez, Project Designer
Maranda Gerga, Project Designer
Jay Williams, Project Designer
Linda Komlos, Administrative Analyst

Fay Jones School of Architecture + Design
Peter MacKeith, Dean and Professor of Architecture
Jennifer Webb, Associate Professor of Interior Design

Department of Architecture Students
Forrest Branam
Kathryn Marie Edwards
Lauren Christine Evans
Caitlyn Juarez
Juan Francisco Martinez
Robert Quinten McElvain
Jonathan Alexander Martinez

National Endowment for the Arts
Sponsor

City of Freeman, South Dakota

Freeman Education and Research, Inc.
John Koch, President
Lyle Preheim, Vice President
Dean Dreessen, Secretary/Treasurer
Tim Waltner
Kelsey Ortman
Anne Waltner
Steve (Charly) Waltner

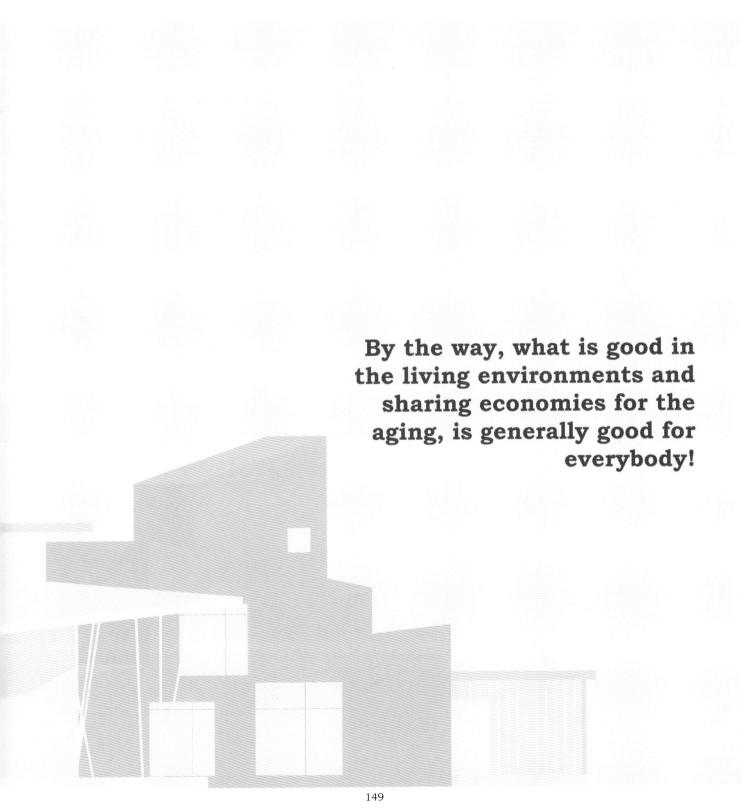

By the way, what is good in the living environments and sharing economies for the aging, is generally good for everybody!

EDITIONS

Publishers of Architecture, Art, and Design
Gordon Goff: Publisher

www.oroeditions.com
info@oroeditions.com

Published by ORO Editions

Graphic Design: University of Arkansas Community Design Center
Edited by: University of Arkansas Community Design Center
Proofread by: Kirby Anderson
Text: University of Arkansas Community Design Center
Project Coordinator: Jake Anderson

10 9 8 7 6 5 4 3 2 1 First Edition

Library of Congress data available upon request. World Rights:
Available

ISBN: 978-1-939621-82-5

Color Separations and Printing: ORO Group Ltd.
Printed in China.

International Distribution: www.oroeditions.com/distribution

ORO Editions makes a continuous effort to minimize the overall
carbon footprint of its publications. As part of this goal, ORO
Editions, in association with Global ReLeaf, arranges to plant trees
to replace those used in the manufacturing of the paper produced
for its books. Global ReLeaf is an international campaign run by
American Forests, one of the world's oldest nonprofit conservation
organizations. Global ReLeaf is American Forests' education and
action program that helps individuals, organizations, agencies, and
corporations improve the local and global environment by planting
and caring for trees.